T H E B O O K O F

FONDUES
V O L U M E 2

LESLEY MAC

PHOTOGRAPHED BY

P A T R I C K M c L E A V E Y

HPBooks

ANOTHER BEST SELLING VOLUME FROM HPBOOKS

HPBooks
Published by the Berkley Publishing Group
A division of Penguin Putnam Inc.
375 Hudson Street
New York, NY 10014

Copyright © 2002 by Salamander Books Ltd.
By arrangement with Salamander Books Ltd.

A member of the Chrysalis Group plc

Project managed by: Stella Caldwell
Photographer: Patrick McLeavey
Designer: Sue Storey
Home Economist: Alex Winsor
Production: Phillip Chamberlain

First edition: February 2002

Visit our website at www.penguinputnam.com

This book has been cataloged with the Library of Congress

ISBN 1-55788-377-7

Printed and bound in Spain

10 9 8 7 6 5 4 3 2 1

CONTENTS

FOREWORD

The fondue is making a huge comeback and sales of fondue sets are rising rapidly, but you do not have to be fresh from the ski slopes to enjoy this fun and informal way of dining. A fondue party is the perfect way to entertain. The simple preparations can be done in advance and the hostess does not need to be stuck in the kitchen but can join the guests at the table as everyone cooks their own dinner!

The Book of Fondues, Volume 2 is packed with over 80 recipes for fondues to suit every occasion. There are classics such as Fondue Savoyarde made with Swiss cheese, Fondue Bourgignonne, and firepots from the Far East. Also included are many exciting new ideas taking their inspiration from all around the world, such as Marrakesh Swordfish Fondue with fragrant North African spices, spicy Cajun Meatballs or Italian Pesto Fondue. There are also suggestions for accompaniments such as salads and sauces.

A large number of the recipes are suitable for vegetarians because they are based on cheese or vegetables, such as Bell Pepper and Tomato Fondue or Wild Mushroom Fondue. Other recipes such as the party fondue with crudités are specifically designed to appeal to children.

Adults and children alike will be tempted by the range of dessert fondues. A pot of melted chocolate with fresh fruit for dipping is an indulgent way to end a meal and could not be simpler to prepare. Banoffee or marshmallow fondues will be popular with anyone with a sweet tooth, and as an alternative to fruit, there are recipes for simple cakes and cookies to dip into the sweet fondues.

The Book of Fondues, Volume 2 also describes the different types of fondue pots available and gives plenty of advice for planning the perfect fondue party.

With *The Book of Fondues, Volume 2* you are sure to find the perfect fondue to suit any occasion and any budget.

INTRODUCTION

The word fondue comes from the French *fondre*, to melt. It was in the French speaking area of Switzerland that the cheese fondue originated many centuries ago. During harsh Alpine winters Swiss peasants had very limited food apart from cheese and bread, and they had few cooking utensils, so melting the cheese in one pot was a good way of using up the rather dry odds and ends of cheese.

The cheese fondue became widely known outside Switzerland when people started taking skiing holiday, and enjoyed a fondue or raclette after a hard day on the slopes.

Many countries have their own version of fondue. The fondue Bourgignonne where strips of steak are cooked in hot oil is popular in France, and in the Far East pieces of meat, fish, or chicken are cooked in boiling stock with vegetables. At the end, noodles are added to the stock which is then served as a soup.

There are many different types of fondue set available. A fondue set usually consists of a pot and burner with a set of four or six long-handled forks. The burner either contains a pad which has to be impregnated with methylated spirits, or a foil container of gel is placed in the burner. They will usually have a sliding cover over

Left: Large stainless steel fondue pot

Right: Cast-iron fondue pot with spirit burner

the burner which will enable you to adjust the size of the flame. A cover is also usually provided for snuffing out the flame when cooking is finished. Small chocolate fondue pots have a candle to provide a gentle heat. The base containing the burner should be very stable and will need to be set on a thick mat on the table. A traditional cheese fondue pot is wide and quite shallow and usually made of earthenware or light metal such as copper. These pots are not suitable for a meat fondue as they are too open and shallow for hot oil or stock. It is quite easy to overheat the metal pots, causing the cheese to catch and burn.

A traditional meat fondue pot is taller and narrower, but most fondue pots sold nowadays tend to be this shape and they are suitable for either meat or cheese fondues. Cast-iron pots tend to be the most expensive but they are the best as it is much easier to keep a steady temperature with cast iron. Another advantage is that the weight of the cast iron sets makes them more stable.

Chocolate fondues are smaller but it is not necessary to have a special pot - an attractive bowl over a night-light candle works well. A chocolate fondue set can also be used for keeping sauces warm at the table. Similar to a chocolate fondue set is a special pot for Bagna Cauda - again, this is heated by a nightlight candle. These are usually made of terracotta.

A Mongolian hotpot or steamboat is a traditional pot for Asian fondues. They are made of brass or aluminum and consist of a rounded pot with a funnel down the center, set over a burner into which hot charcoal is placed. Hot stock is used and the burner keeps it bubbling throughout the meal.

Long-handled forks are essential for spearing whatever is being dipped into the fondue. They usually have colored handles or a colored mark on the end so that each diner can identify his or her fork. The food is transferred to a table fork before eating, not just for hygiene reasons, but to avoid burning - particularly important when dipping

Above: Small chocolate fondue pot

into hot oil. As an alternative to forks, bamboo skewers may be used. Little Chinese wire baskets are used with Mongolian hotpots but they are also useful for dipping meatballs, fishcakes, or anything else which might be too fragile to stay on a fork.

Six is the maximum number of people who can safely and comfortably share one fondue pot, so for parties of eight or more it would be necessary to have two pots on the go. For speed, make the cheese fondue on top of the stove before transferring it to the burner. Also heat oil or stock on top of the stove and take great care when transferring the fondue pot to the burner.

CHEESE FONDUES

Choose a strongly flavored cheese and always allow it to melt slowly. You need alcohol in a cheese fondue. Not only does it add flavor, but it lowers the boiling point and stops the protein in the cheese curdling. Do not worry if the mixture looks lumpy and separates; keep stirring and it will gradually become smooth, but do not be tempted to turn the heat up. If it becomes too thick add a little warmed wine or cider. Encourage diners to stir

the fondue right down to the bottom when they dip their bread in, this helps to keep it smooth and creamy. When the fondue is nearly finished there will be a crisp crust on the bottom off the pot. Scrape it out and divide it between the guests - it is regarded as a great treat.

Use day-old bread for dipping as it will not be too crumbly, and always cut the bread so that each piece has some crust on for spearing with the fork. If anybody does drop their bread in the fondue they have to perform a forfeit. Traditionally ladies have to kiss the man next to them and a man has to buy the next round of drinks!

MEAT, FISH, AND SEAFOOD FONDUES

It is important to have all the ingredients and accompaniments prepared in advance. The meat should be cut and arranged attractively on plates, sauces should be prepared and served in small pots, and salads should be ready to be dressed just before the cooking begins. If using oil, use a vegetable oil, but a little flavored oil can be added if desired. The fondue pot should not be filled more than half full as the hot oil can bubble up a bit when the meat is

dipped in. The oil should be heated to 350-375F (180-190C), but if you do not have a thermometer, test it with a piece of day-old bread. A small cube will turn golden in about 30 seconds if the oil is at the correct temperature. Do not add too much food to the oil at once. This will lower the temperature of the oil and the food will not cook properly. Meat and fish should be thoroughly dried on paper towels before cooking in the hot oil, otherwise the oil will spit.

DESSERT FONDUES
Most dessert fondues are made of chocolate, but creamy fruit purées are popular too. Take great care when melting the chocolate, especially white chocolate, as it will solidify into clumps if it is overheated. Melting the chocolate with cream solves the problem.

If you are dipping cake into the fondue, make sure it is not too crumbly. Day-old cake works best. If you are dipping fruit, choose firm pieces and, if possible, chill them first and the chocolate will coat them more easily.

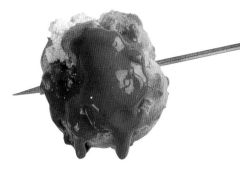

— CARIBBEAN FISH FONDUE —

2 teaspoons hot pepper sauce
2 teaspoons soft brown sugar
1 teaspoon crushed allspice
1 clove garlic, crushed
½ teaspoon ground coriander
juice 1 lime
1½lb cod loin
2½ cups coconut milk
1 Scotch bonnet chili
salt
MANGO SALSA
1 mango, peeled and finely diced
½ small red onion, finely diced
1 fresh red chili, cored, seeded, and finely chopped
3 tablespoons chopped fresh cilantro
grated rind and juice 1 lime

In a bowl, mix together hot pepper sauce, sugar, allspice, garlic, coriander, and lime juice. Cut fish into cubes and add to the bowl. Stir to coat in the marinade, cover, and leave in a cool place for 30 minutes. (See above.) Meanwhile, make the mango salsa. In a bowl, mix together mango, onion, chili, cilantro, and lime rind and juice. Set aside. Remove the fish from the marinade, drain, and arrange on a serving plate.

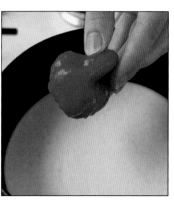

Heat the coconut milk and Scotch bonnet chili in the fondue pot on top of the stove. Season with salt then transfer to the lighted spirit burner. Spear the fish on to the fondue forks and cook in the hot coconut milk for 2-3 minutes. Serve with the mango salsa.

Serves 4

SHRIMP IN JACKETS

2 sheets filo pastry approximately 18x10 inch
2 tablespoons butter, melted
9oz (approximately 32) large raw shrimp, peeled and
  thawed if frozen
salt and freshly ground black pepper
oil, for cooking
WASABI MAYONNAISE
⅔ cup mayonnaise
1 teaspoon wasabi paste
2 teaspoons lime juice

Make the wasabi mayonnaise. In a bowl, mix together mayonnaise, wasabi paste, and lime juice. Set aside.

Lightly brush sheets of filo pastry with melted butter. Cut each sheet into strips across. The strips should be as wide as the shrimp are long. Cut each strip in half across. Dry shrimp on paper towels and season with salt and pepper. Roll a strip of pastry round each shrimp and arrange on a serving dish.

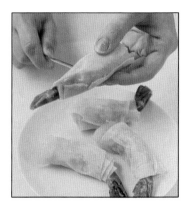

Heat the oil in the fondue pot on top of the stove then transfer to the lighted spirit burner. Spear the wrapped shrimp on the fondue forks and cook in the hot oil for 2 minutes or until crisp and golden. Serve with the wasabi mayonnaise.

Serves 4

SEAFOOD FONDUE

8oz raw jumbo shrimp
2½ cups good fish stock
½ lemon, sliced
1 small onion, peeled
8oz monkfish, skinned
8oz thick cod fillet, skinned
8oz scallops
lemon wedges and parsley sprigs, to garnish
Rouille (see page 86), to serve

Peel the shrimp and place the shells in a saucepan with the stock, lemon, and onion. Bring to a boil and simmer for 10 minutes.

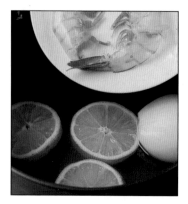

Cut monkfish and cod into cubes and halve the scallops if they are large. Arrange on serving plates with the peeled shrimp. Garnish with lemon wedges and parsley sprigs. Cover and keep cool.

Strain stock into the fondue pot, bring back to a boil on top of the stove, then transfer to the lighted spirit burner. Spear the fish on to the fondue forks and cook in the hot stock for 2-3 minutes. Serve with Rouille.

Serves 6

VARIATION: The selection of fish can be varied according to personal preference and what is available.

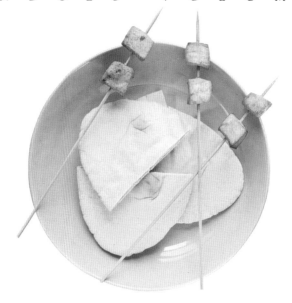

MARRAKESH SWORDFISH FONDUE

1 small red onion, finely chopped
2 cloves garlic, crushed
1 fresh red chili, cored, seeded, and finely chopped
2 tablespoons chopped fresh cilantro
1 tablespoon chopped fresh mint
1 teaspoon ground cumin
1 teaspoon paprika
pinch saffron strands
4 tablespoons olive oil
juice 1 lemon
salt
1½lb swordfish, skinned
oil, for cooking
green salad and warm pita bread, to serve

In a bowl, mix together the onion, garlic, chili, cilantro, mint, cumin, paprika, saffron, olive oil, lemon juice, and salt. (See above.) Cut monkfish into cubes. Add them to spice mixture in the bowl. Mix well to coat, cover, and leave in a cool place for 1 hour.

Using a slotted spoon, remove fish from the bowl and arrange on a serving plate. Heat oil in the fondue pot on top of the stove then transfer to the lighted spirit burner. Spear fish on to the fondue forks and cook in the hot oil for 2-3 minutes. Serve with salad and warm pita bread.

Serves 4

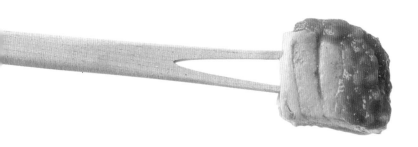

NIÇOISE FONDUE

1 tablespoon olive oil
1 onion, finely chopped
2 cloves garlic, crushed
14oz can chopped tomatoes
½ cup dry white wine
1 teaspoon dried herbes de Provence
3½oz canned or bottled anchovies, drained
2 tablespoons pitted olives, chopped
salt and freshly ground black pepper
12oz cooked French beans, halved
3 hard boiled eggs, quartered
4 tablespoons vinaigrette dressing
1lb fresh tuna fish
French bread, to serve

Heat the oil in a pan, add onion and garlic, and cook gently for 10 minutes or until soft. Add tomatoes, white wine, ⅓ cup water, and herbes de Provence and simmer gently for about 10 minutes until well blended. (See above.) Process in a blender or food processor to make a smooth sauce, then add anchovies and olives, and process briefly until finely chopped. Season with salt and pepper and pour into the fondue pot.

Combine beans and eggs with vinaigrette dressing and place in a serving dish. Cut tuna fish into cubes and arrange on a serving dish. Heat tomato sauce on top of the stove until simmering then transfer to the lighted spirit burner. Spear cubes of tuna fish on fondue forks and cook in the hot tomato sauce for 2 minutes or until cooked as desired. Serve with the bean and egg salad and French bread.

Serves 4

PIRI PIRI SHRIMP

1 fresh red chili, cored, seeded, and very finely
  chopped
½ teaspoon paprika
½ teaspoon ground coriander
1 clove garlic, crushed
finely grated rind 1 lime
salt and freshly ground black pepper
9oz large raw shrimp, peeled and thawed if frozen
oil, for cooking
lime wedges, to garnish
Aioli (see page 88) and bread, to serve

In a bowl, mix together chili, paprika,
ground coriander, garlic, lime rind, salt, and
pepper.

Add shrimp and mix well. Cover and leave
in a cool place for 30 minutes. Heat the oil
in the fondue pot on top of the stove then
transfer to the lighted spirit burner.

Thread shrimp on to fondue forks or
bamboo skewers and cook in the hot oil for
1 minute or until pink. Serve, garnished
with lime wedges, with the aioli and bread.

Serves 4

BAGNA CAUDA

¼ cup butter
4 cloves garlic, crushed
2oz can anchovy fillets, drained and roughly chopped
⅔ cup mild extra virgin olive oil
TO SERVE
a selection of raw and blanched vegetables such as
    celery, carrots, fennel, bell peppers, radishes,
    asparagus, cauliflower, baby artichoke hearts
hard boiled quails' eggs
breadsticks
toasted cubes of ciabatta bread

Arrange vegetables, eggs, and bread on serving plates.

Gently heat butter in a heavy saucepan. Add garlic and cook gently, for 2 minutes. Add anchovies, then pour in oil very slowly, stirring constantly. Cook gently, stirring, for about 10 minutes. Do not allow to boil. The sauce in ready when anchovies have become a paste.

Transfer sauce to an earthenware bagna cauda pot or a fondue pot and place over the lighted spirit burner. To serve, dip vegetables, eggs, and bread into the anchovy sauce.

Serves 4-6

— CRISPY CRUMBED MUSSELS —

2¼lb fresh mussels in shells
2 lemons, quartered
6 cloves garlic, peeled
2 eggs, beaten
2 cups fresh bread crumbs
oil, for cooking
lemon wedges, to garnish
Rouille (see page 86), to serve

Scrub mussels and remove the beards. Discard any which do not close when tapped sharply. Place mussels in a large pan with lemon quarters and garlic. Add 4 tablespoons water to the pan.

Cover and cook on a high heat for a few minutes, shaking pan occasionally until mussels open. Discard any which remain closed. Drain mussels and remove from shells. Dry on paper towels. Place beaten egg and bread crumbs in 2 separate shallow dishes. Dip the mussels into egg, allowing the excess to drip back, then dip in bread crumbs. Place on a serving dish.

Heat the oil in the fondue pot on top of the stove then transfer to the lighted spirit burner. Thread the mussels, two at a time, on to fondue forks or bamboo skewers and cook in the hot oil for 1 minute or until crisp and golden. Serve, garnished with lemon wedges, with the rouille.

Serves 4

VARIATION: For a quick version of this dish, ready prepared breaded mussels, squid, or scampi could be used.

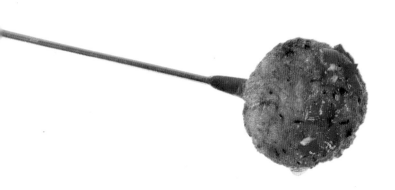

THAI FISH CAKES

1lb boneless cod fillet
2 tablespoons chopped fresh cilantro
1 tablespoon Thai red curry paste
1 small egg, beaten
1 teaspoon soft brown sugar
1 tablespoon cornstarch
1 teaspoon salt
oil, for cooking
lime wedges, to garnish
CHILI DIPPING SAUCE
4 tablespoons rice vinegar
4 tablespoons soy sauce
1 teaspoon soft brown sugar
1 clove garlic, crushed
1 fresh red chili, cored, seeded, and finely chopped
1 teaspoon sesame oil

Cut cod into chunks and chop roughly in a food processor. Add chopped cilantro, curry paste, egg, sugar, cornstarch, and salt. Process again until well blended. Chill the mixture for 30 minutes. Divide mixture into 16 pieces, roll each into a ball, then flatten slightly into a cake. Place on a serving dish and chill. (See above.) Make the dipping sauce. Place vinegar, soy sauce, sugar, garlic, chili, and sesame oil in a bowl and whisk together. Divide between small serving bowls.

Heat oil in the fondue pot on top of the stove then transfer to the lighted spirit burner. To cook the fishcakes, place them in wire baskets and dip into hot oil for 2-3 minutes until golden and cooked through. Serve, garnished with lime wedges, with the dipping sauce.

Serves 4

FISH FIREPOT

1½lb assorted boneless skinless fish such as salmon,
 cod, and monkfish
8oz large raw peeled shrimp or scallops or a mixture
 of both
1lb pak choi, cut into thin strips
8oz button mushrooms, halved
7oz fine egg noodles, cooked
chopped fresh cilantro
7½ cups fish stock
3 tablespoons rice wine or dry sherry
1 teaspoon salt
DIPPING SAUCE
1 fresh red chili, cored, seeded, and finely chopped
2 cloves garlic, crushed
4 tablespoons soy sauce
1 tablespoon tamarind paste

Cut fish into thin slices and halve scallops if
they are large. (See above.) Arrange fish on
4 or 6 individual serving plates. Cover and
chill until required. Arrange pak choi,
mushrooms, and noodles on serving plates.
Place chopped cilantro in a shallow dish.
Make dipping sauce. In a bowl, mix together
chili, garlic, soy sauce, and tamarind paste.
If using a Mongolian hotpot, light it and
place on the table. Pour in stock and add
rice wine or sherry and salt. Bring to a boil.

(If using a fondue pot, pour stock and rice
wine or sherry into the pot, add salt, and
bring to a boil on the stove. Transfer to the
lighted spirit burner.) Dip pieces of fish into
stock, using chopsticks or Chinese wire
strainers. Remove from stock and dip into
sauce or cilantro before eating. From time to
time add mushrooms and pak choi to the
stock, and when cooked remove and eat.
Finally, add noodles to stock to heat through,
then serve the soup in warmed bowls.

Serves 6

MANHATTAN FONDUE

8-10 bagels
4oz smoked salmon
1¼ cups cream cheese
¼ cup milk
1 tablespoon chopped fresh dill
salt and freshly ground black pepper

Split the bagels, toast lightly, and cut into bite-size pieces. Divide between 4-6 serving plates.

Chop smoked salmon into small pieces. Place cream cheese and milk in the fondue pot and heat gently on the stove until cheese has melted to a smooth sauce.

Stir in the dill and smoked salmon, and season with salt and a generous amount of black pepper. Transfer the pot to the lighted spirit burner and keep warm over a low heat. Spear the pieces of bagel on fondue forks and dip into the sauce.

Serves 4-6

SMOKED FISH GOUJONS

4 heaping tablespoons all-purpose flour
salt and freshly ground black pepper
1½lb skinless and boneless smoked fish fillets
3 eggs, beaten
2 cups fresh bread crumbs
oil, for cooking
lemon wedges, to garnish
REMOULADE SAUCE
⅔ cup mayonnaise
1 teaspoon Dijon mustard
2 teaspoons finely chopped capers
2 teaspoons finely chopped gherkins
2 teaspoons finely chopped fresh tarragon

To make the sauce mix together the mayonnaise, mustard, capers, gherkins, and tarragon. Set aside. (See above.) Place flour in a shallow dish. Season with salt and pepper and mix together. Cut fish into strips about ½ inch wide. Dust strips with seasoned flour. Place beaten egg and bread crumbs in 2 separate shallow dishes. Dip each piece of fish in the egg allowing the excess to drip back in, then dip in bread crumbs. Place on a serving dish.

Heat oil in the fondue pot on top of the stove then transfer to the lighted spirit burner. Spear fish on to fondue forks and cook in oil for 1-2 minutes until crisp and golden. Serve, garnished with lemon wedges, with the sauce.

Serves 4

— ANCHOVY & SHRIMP FONDUE —

2oz anchovy fillets, drained
1 clove garlic, halved
⅔ cup dry white wine
1 cup grated Gruyère cheese
2 cups grated Cheddar cheese
1 teaspoon cornstarch
2 tablespoons dry sherry
Tabasco sauce
TO SERVE
8oz large peeled cooked shrimp
cubes of French bread

Place anchovy fillets in a mortar and pound to a paste with the pestle. Arrange shrimp and bread on serving plates.

Rub inside of a fondue pot with cut clove of garlic. Pour in wine and heat gently on the stove until bubbling. Gradually stir in both cheeses. Heat gently, stirring, until the cheese has melted. In a small bowl, blend cornstarch with the sherry.

Stir cornstarch mixture into cheese and add Tabasco sauce, to taste, and anchovy paste. Cook gently, stirring until thick and creamy. Transfer pot to the lighted spirit burner. Serve with the shrimp and bread.

Serves 4-6

— SWEET & SOUR FISH FONDUE —

2 eggs
1 cup all-purpose flour
1½lb boneless skinless firm white fish such as
   monkfish, cut into cubes
oil, for cooking
SWEET & SOUR SAUCE
1 tablespoon oil
1 small onion, finely chopped
1 green bell pepper, seeded and sliced
1 teaspoon cornstarch
2 tablespoons soft brown sugar
2 tablespoons white wine vinegar
2 tablespoons tomato paste
juice 1 small orange
2 tablespoons soy sauce
2 tablespoons finely chopped pineapple

To make sauce, heat the oil in a saucepan.
Add onion and cook for 5 minutes until
beginning to soften. Add bell pepper and
cook for 5 more minutes. In a small bowl,
blend cornstarch with 4 tablespoons water
and add to the pan with sugar, vinegar,
tomato paste, orange juice, soy sauce, and
pineapple. Bring to a boil, stirring, and cook
until the sauce thickens. Keep warm.

Make the batter; whisk eggs with scant
1 cup iced water until frothy. Add flour and
beat until just blended. Divide between
6 small bowls. Divide the fish between
6 serving plates. Heat oil in the fondue pot
on top of the stove then transfer to the
lighted spirit burner. Spear the fish on to
the fondue forks, dip in the batter, then in
hot oil for 2-3 minutes until batter is crisp
and golden. Serve with the sweet and sour
sauce.

Serves 6

— FONDUE BOURGIGNONNE —

2¼lb lean fillet or rump steak
oil, for cooking
small baked potatoes and green salad, to serve
  (optional)
SAUCES
2½ cups mayonnaise
2oz anchovies, drained
2 tablespoons horseradish sauce
2 tablespoons tomato paste
2 teaspoons hot pepper sauce
1 tablespoon curry paste

Cut steak into 1 inch cubes and arrange on
4-6 serving plates.

To make the sauces, divide mayonnaise
between 4 bowls. Using a mortar and pestle,
pound anchovies to a puree, and stir into
one of the bowls of mayonnaise. Stir
horseradish sauce into another, tomato
paste and hot pepper sauce into another,
and curry paste into the last bowl. Transfer
sauces to small serving bowls.

Heat oil in the fondue pot on top of the
stove then transfer to the lighted spirit
burner. Spear steak on to fondue forks and
cook in hot oil according to individual taste.
Serve with the sauces, and baked potatoes
and salad, if you like.

Serves 6

VARIATIONS: Lean fillet of lamb could be
served instead of or as well as the steak.

CAJUN MEATBALLS

1 tablespoon oil
1 onion, finely chopped
1 teaspoon coriander seeds
½ teaspoon cardamom seeds
1lb lean ground steak
1 cup fresh bread crumbs
1 small egg, beaten
grated rind ½ lemon
¼-½ teaspoon chili powder
2 tablespoons chopped fresh cilantro
salt and freshly ground black pepper
oil, for cooking
TO SERVE
Chili Tomato Sauce (see page 87)
pita bread
shredded lettuce

Heat oil in a saucepan. Add onion and cook for 10 minutes until soft. Set aside to cool. In a small heavy based saucepan, dry fry coriander and cardamom seeds for a few minutes until golden, then crush, using a mortar and pestle. In a bowl, mix together the onion, ground steak, crushed spices, bread crumbs, egg, lemon rind, chili powder, cilantro, and salt and pepper until thoroughly combined.

Form the mixture into walnut-size balls. Arrange on serving plates and chill until required. Heat oil in the fondue pot on top of the stove then transfer to the lighted spirit burner. Spear meatballs on to the fondue forks and cook in the hot oil for 3-4 minutes until cooked. Serve with the sauce, pita bread and lettuce.

Serves 4-6

KOFTAS & RAITA

1 small onion, roughly chopped
1 clove garlic, chopped
1 inch piece fresh root ginger, peeled and chopped
1 teaspoon ground cumin
1 teaspoon ground coriander
1 tablespoon oil
1lb lean ground lamb
3 tablespoons chopped fresh cilantro
salt and freshly ground black pepper
1 small egg, beaten
oil, for cooking
naan bread or chapatis, to serve
RAITA
½ cucumber
1½ cups Greek-style yogurt
3 tablespoons chopped fresh mint

Put onion, garlic, and ginger in a blender or food processor and chop finely, without turning to a paste. Add cumin and ground coriander, and process briefly to blend. Heat oil in a skillet, add onion mixture, and cook for 2-3 minutes, stirring. (See above.) Leave to cool. In a bowl, mix together ground lamb, cilantro, seasoning, and cooled onion mixture. Mix thoroughly. Add just enough beaten egg to bind mixture together. With floured hands, roll mixture into bite-size balls. Arrange on serving plates and chill until required.

To make the raita, grate cucumber coarsely. Squeeze out as much liquid as possible then mix cucumber, yogurt, and mint together. Season with salt and pepper, and transfer to small serving bowls. Heat oil in the fondue pot on top of the stove then transfer to the lighted spirit burner. Spear the koftas on to fondue forks and cook in the hot oil for 3-4 minutes until cooked. Serve with the raita and naan bread or chapatis.

Serves 4-6

TURKISH LAMB

1½lb lean lamb
2 cloves garlic, crushed
4 tablespoons lemon juice
pinch chili powder
1 teaspoon ground cumin
1 teaspoon ground coriander
½ teaspoon ground cinnamon
salt and freshly ground black pepper
oil, for cooking
TO SERVE
Tomato and Olive Salsa (see page 90)
pita bread

Cut the lamb into 1 inch cubes.

Crush garlic and place in a bowl. Add lemon juice, chili powder, cumin, ground coriander, and cinnamon, and stir. Add lamb and mix until well coated with marinade. Cover and leave to marinate in a cool place for 2 hours.

Remove lamb from marinade and pat dry with paper towels. Season with salt and pepper. Arrange the lamb on 4 serving plates. Heat the oil in the fondue pot on top of the stove then transfer to the lighted spirit burner. Spear the lamb on to fondue forks and cook in the hot oil for 3-4 minutes until cooked. Serve with the tomato and olive salsa.

Serves 4

PORK SATAY

1 teaspoon tamarind paste
2 cloves garlic, crushed
2 tablespoons soy sauce
1 teaspoon ground cumin
1 teaspoon ground coriander
½ teaspoon chili powder
salt
1lb lean pork steaks
oil, for cooking
SATAY SAUCE
2 tablespoons smooth peanut butter
scant 1 cup coconut cream
2 teaspoons red Thai curry paste
1 tablespoon fish sauce
1 tablespoon soft brown sugar

In a bowl mix together tamarind paste, garlic, soy sauce, ground cumin, ground coriander, chili, and salt. (See above.) Place pork steaks between 2 pieces of plastic wrap and beat out flat with a meat hammer or rolling pin. Cut into strips then place in the bowl with marinade. Mix well then cover and leave in a cool place for 1 hour. Remove from marinade, dry with paper towels, and thread on to bamboo skewers. Arrange on serving plates.

To make satay sauce, place peanut butter, coconut cream, red curry paste, fish sauce, and brown sugar in a pan. Heat gently to form a smooth sauce, adding a little water if necessary. Keep warm. Heat oil in the fondue pot on top of the stove then transfer to the lighted spirit burner. Cook the skewers of pork in the hot oil for 3-4 minutes until cooked. Serve with the satay sauce.

Serves 4

– MEXICAN BEEF & GUACAMOLE –

1½lb sirloin or rump steak
2 teaspoons chili sauce
2 cloves garlic, crushed
1 tablespoon chopped fresh cilantro
1 teaspoon dried oregano
1 teaspoon ground cumin
juice 1 lime
tortilla chips, to serve
GUACAMOLE
2-3 ripe avocados, depending on the size
½ red onion, finely chopped
1 tablespoon chopped fresh cilantro
1 clove garlic, crushed
1 red chili, cored, seeded, and finely chopped
2 tomatoes, peeled, seeded and finely chopped
juice ½ -1 lime
pinch sugar
salt and freshly ground black pepper

Cut steak into 1 inch cubes. In a bowl, mix together chili sauce, garlic, cilantro, oregano, cumin, and lime juice. Add steak and mix well. (See above.) Cover and marinate in the refrigerator for 1-2 hours. Meanwhile, make guacamole. Peel and pit avocados, place in a bowl, and mash with a fork. Do not make mixture too smooth. Stir in onion, cilantro, garlic, chili, and tomato. Then stir in lime juice, sugar, and salt and pepper to taste.

Leave to stand for 30 minutes, but no longer than 1 hour. Just before serving, stir again and transfer to small serving bowls. Remove steak from marinade, dry with paper towels, and arrange on serving plates. Heat oil in the fondue pot on top of the stove then transfer to the lighted spirit burner. Spear cubes of steak on to fondue forks and cook in hot oil for 3-4 minutes until cooked. Serve with guacamole and tortilla chips.

Serves 4-6

TERIYAKI STEAK

1½lb fillet steak
2 inch piece fresh root ginger
1 tablespoon oil
1 clove garlic, crushed
4 tablespoons soy sauce
2 tablespoons mirin or medium sherry
1 teaspoon soft light brown sugar
freshly ground black pepper
TO SERVE
1 daikon radish
2 tablespoons wasabi paste
cilantro sprigs

Cut the steaks into thin strips ½ inch wide and 4 inch long.

Peel ginger and grate into a bowl. Squeeze out liquid and put 1 tablespoon in a dish with oil, garlic, soy sauce, mirin or sherry, and sugar. Add steak, mix well, cover, and leave to marinate in the refrigerator for 1 hour. Meanwhile, prepare garnish. Peel daikon radish and grate into a bowl. Squeeze out as much liquid as possible and divide the grated daikon radish between 4 serving plates. Place a little wasabi paste and a sprig of cilantro on each plate.

Remove steak from marinade and pat dry with paper towels. Season with pepper. Thread strips of steak on to bamboo skewers and divide between 4 serving dishes. Heat oil in the fondue pot on top of the stove then transfer to the lighted spirit burner. Cook the steak in hot oil for 2-3 minutes until cooked. Serve with daikon radish and wasabi, garnished with cilantro.

Serves 4

— CURRIED APRICOT TURKEY —

1 tablespoon oil
1 onion, finely chopped
1 clove garlic, crushed
2 bay leaves
juice 1 lemon
2 tablespoons curry powder
4 tablespoons apricot jam
4 tablespoons apple juice
salt
1½lb turkey fillet
4 tablespoons crème fraîche
oil, for cooking

Heat oil in a saucepan. Add onion, garlic, and bay leaves and cook for 10 minutes until soft.

Add lemon juice, curry powder, apricot jam, apple juice, and salt to taste. Cook gently for 5 minutes. Transfer to a bowl and leave to cool. Cut turkey into 1 inch cubes and add to cooled marinade. Mix well, cover and leave to marinate in the refrigerator for 2 hours.

Remove turkey and allow marinade to run back into the bowl. Dry turkey with paper towels and arrange on 4 serving plates. Transfer marinade to a pan and simmer for 2 minutes. Stir in crème fraîche. Heat oil in the fondue pot on top of the stove then transfer to the lighted spirit burner. Spear turkey on to fondue forks and cook in hot oil for 3-4 minutes until cooked. Serve with the sauce.

Serves 4

PROVENÇAL BEEF

2 cloves garlic, crushed
⅔ cup red wine
grated rind and juice ½ orange
1 tablespoon chopped fresh rosemary
1 teaspoon dried herbes de provence
2 tablespoons olive oil
1¼lb rump or fillet steak
salt and freshly ground black pepper
oil, for cooking
TOMATO SALAD
1lb tomatoes, sliced
6 scallions, thinly sliced
2 tablespoons shredded basil leaves
1 clove garlic, crushed
6 tablespoons olive oil
2 tablespoons balsamic vinegar

In a bowl, mix together garlic, wine, orange rind and juice, rosemary, herbes de provence, and olive oil. Cut steak into 1 inch cubes and add to marinade. Cover and marinate overnight in the refrigerator. Meanwhile, make salad. Arrange sliced tomatoes on individual serving plates. Sprinkle scallions and basil over tomatoes. In a small bowl, whisk together garlic, olive oil, balsamic vinegar, and salt and pepper. Pour over tomatoes, cover, and leave to marinate for 1 hour.

Remove steak from marinade and dry on paper towels. Season with salt and pepper and arrange on serving plates. Heat oil in the fondue pot on top of the stove then transfer to the lighted spirit burner. Spear the steak on to fondue forks and cook in hot oil for 3-4 minutes until cooked. Serve with the tomato salad.

Serves 4

JERK CHICKEN

grated rind and juice 1 lime
1 inch piece fresh root ginger
3 tablespoons olive oil
1 clove garlic, crushed
1 teaspoon dried thyme
1 teaspoon ground cinnamon
1 teaspoon ground allspice
1 teaspoon soft brown sugar
2 teaspoons hot pepper sauce
salt and freshly ground black pepper
2lb skinless, boneless chicken breast
lime wedges, to garnish
oil, for frying
Bean Salad (see page 92), to serve

Grate rind from lime and squeeze juice into a bowl. Peel ginger and grate into the bowl. Add olive oil, garlic, thyme, cinnamon, allspice, sugar, hot pepper sauce, and salt and pepper. Mix together. (See above.) Cut chicken into 1 inch cubes and add to marinade. Cover and leave in a cool place to marinate for 2 hours.

Remove chicken from marinade, pat dry with paper towels, and arrange on serving plates. Garnish with lime wedges. Heat oil in the fondue pot on top of the stove then transfer to the lighted spirit burner. Spear chicken on to fondue forks and cook in hot oil for 3-4 minutes until cooked. Serve with the salad.

Serves 6

CHICKEN TIKKA

2 inch piece fresh root ginger
4 tablespoons plain yogurt
1-2 tablespoons hot Madras curry paste
2 cloves garlic, crushed
1 teaspoon turmeric
2 tablespoons lemon juice
1 teaspoon paprika
½ teaspoon salt
1½lb skinless, boneless chicken breast
cilantro sprigs and lemon wedges, to garnish
oil, for cooking
TO SERVE
Raita (see page 28)
naan bread
poppadoms

Peel ginger and grate into a bowl. Add the yogurt, curry paste, garlic, turmeric, lemon juice, paprika, and salt. Mix together thoroughly. (See above.) Cut chicken into ¾ inch cubes. Add to marinade and mix well. Cover and leave in the refrigerator to marinate for at least 2 hours. Remove from marinade and allow as much of the marinade to drain off as possible.

Thread chicken cubes, 2 or 3 together, on to bamboo skewers and arrange on serving plates, garnished with cilantro and lemon wedges. Heat oil in the fondue pot on top of the stove then transfer to the lighted spirit burner. Cook chicken in hot oil for 3-4 minutes until cooked. Serve with the raita, naan bread, and poppadoms.

Serves 4

FIVE-SPICE DUCK

3-4 duck breast halves, about 1½lb total weight
1 teaspoon sesame oil
3 tablespoons soy sauce
3 tablespoons rice wine or dry sherry
1 tablespoon honey
1 tablespoon lime juice
2 teaspoons five-spice powder
1 clove garlic, crushed
1 inch piece fresh root ginger, grated
lime wedges, to garnish
oil, for cooking
TO SERVE
shredded scallions
shredded celery
hoisin or plum sauce
Chinese pancakes or flour tortillas

Remove skin and fat from duck breast halves and cut meat into thin strips. Place in a shallow dish. In a bowl, mix together sesame oil, soy sauce, rice wine or sherry, honey, lime juice, five-spice powder, garlic, and ginger. (See above.) Pour over duck and stir well. Cover and leave in a cool place to marinate for 30 minutes. Remove duck strips from marinade and dry on paper towels. Arrange on serving plates and garnish with lime wedges. Arrange scallions and celery on serving plates and place hoisin or plum sauce in small bowls.

Warm Chinese pancakes or tortillas and keep warm. Heat oil in the fondue pot on top of the stove then transfer to the lighted spirit burner. Spear strips of duck on to fondue forks, or thread on to bamboo skewers. Cook in hot oil for 3-4 minutes until cooked. To serve, spread a little hoisin or plum sauce on a pancake or tortilla, add some scallion and celery, and place a few strips of cooked duck on top then roll up.

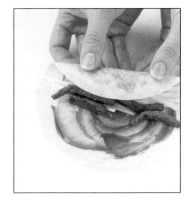

Serves 4-6

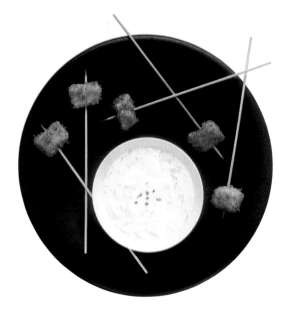

TURKEY NUGGETS

1½lb turkey fillets
3 tablespoons all-purpose flour
salt and freshly ground black pepper
1 cup dry bread crumbs
2 teaspoons finely grated lemon rind
2 extra large eggs, beaten
lemon wedges, to garnish
oil, for frying
HERB DIP
1 cup fromage frais
1 clove garlic, crushed
2 tablespoons chopped fresh tarragon
1 tablespoon chopped fresh chives
1 tablespoon chopped fresh chervil
salt and freshly ground black pepper

Cut turkey into bite-size cubes. In a bowl, mix together flour, salt, and pepper. In a shallow dish, mix together bread crumbs and lemon rind. Pour beaten egg into another shallow dish. Toss turkey cubes in seasoned flour, dip in beaten egg, then coat in bread crumbs. (See above.) Arrange on serving plates and garnish with lemon wedges. To make herb dip, place fromage frais in a bowl, add garlic, tarragon, chives, and chervil, and season with salt and pepper. Mix well together then divide between small serving bowls.

Heat oil in the fondue pot on top of the stove then transfer to the lighted spirit burner. Spear turkey nuggets on to fondue forks and cook in hot oil for 3-4 minutes until cooked. Serve with the herb dip.

Serves 4-6

VARIATION: Chicken may be used as an alternative to turkey.

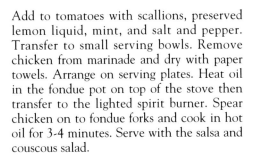

HARISSA-SPICED CHICKEN

2 teaspoons coriander seeds
1½ teaspoons cumin seeds
2 cloves garlic
1-2 tablespoons chili paste
½ teaspoon salt
4 tablespoons olive oil
1½lb skinless, boneless chicken breast
oil, for cooking
Couscous Salad (see page 93), to serve
TOMATO & PRESERVED LEMON SALSA
3-4 ripe tomatoes
½ preserved lemon
2 scallions, chopped
2 tablespoons liquid from the preserved lemons
1 tablespoon chopped fresh mint
salt and freshly ground black pepper

Heat a heavy based skillet. Add coriander and cumin seeds, and dry fry, stirring, for 2 or 3 minutes until they give off a fragrant aroma. (See above.) Grind to a powder using a mortar and pestle. Place ground seeds in a bowl with garlic, chili paste, salt, and olive oil. Mix together. Cut chicken into cubes and add to marinade. Cover and leave in the refrigerator for 1 hour. Make the salsa. Cut tomatoes into dice and place in a bowl. Remove flesh from preserved lemon and cut skin into dice.

Add to tomatoes with scallions, preserved lemon liquid, mint, and salt and pepper. Transfer to small serving bowls. Remove chicken from marinade and dry with paper towels. Arrange on serving plates. Heat oil in the fondue pot on top of the stove then transfer to the lighted spirit burner. Spear chicken on to fondue forks and cook in hot oil for 3-4 minutes. Serve with the salsa and couscous salad.

Serves 4

— THAI CHICKEN MEATBALLS —

1lb ground chicken
4 scallions, chopped
2 tablespoons chopped fresh cilantro
2 tablespoons Thai green curry paste
1 teaspoon soft brown sugar
1 teaspoon salt
lime wedges, to garnish
oil, for cooking
DIPPING SAUCE
1 fresh red chili, cored, seeded, and finely chopped
2 tablespoons light soy sauce
1 tablespoons Thai fish sauce
1 tablespoon lime juice
2 tablespoons soft brown sugar

In a bowl, mix together chicken, scallions, cilantro, curry paste, sugar, and salt. (See above.) Form into small balls. Cover and chill for 30 minutes. Make the dipping sauce. Place chili, soy sauce, fish sauce, lime juice, and sugar in a bowl and mix together. Divide between 4 small dip dishes.

Arrange chicken balls on serving plates and garnish with lime wedges. Heat oil in the fondue pot on top of the stove then transfer to the lighted spirit burner. Spear chicken balls on to fondue forks and cook in hot oil for 3-4 minutes. Serve with the dipping sauce.

Serves 4

THAI CHICKEN HOTPOT

2lb skinless, boneless chicken breast
12 button mushrooms
12 scallions, cut into 2 inch lengths
1 red bell pepper, seeded and cut into strips
4oz baby corn
4oz snow peas
1 bunch watercress
4oz fine egg noodles, broken into pieces
3¼ cups good chicken stock
2 small red chilies
3 kaffir lime leaves
1 stalk lemon grass, crushed
2 slices fresh galangal or ginger
1 carrot, cut into thin matchsticks
6 Chinese leaves, shredded
dipping sauce (see page 40), to serve

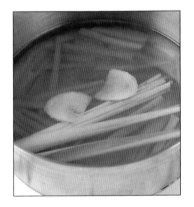

Cut chicken into thin strips, place on 6 serving plates, cover, and chill until required. Divide mushrooms, scallions, bell pepper, corn, snow peas, and watercress between 6 plates, cover, and chill until required. Soak the egg noodles in boiling water for 3-4 minutes, then drain and transfer to a serving bowl. (See above.) Place stock in a saucepan or fondue pot. Add chilies, lime leaves, lemon grass, and galangal or ginger. Bring to a boil and simmer gently for 10 minutes. Add carrot.

Either transfer stock to a hot pot or transfer the fondue pot to the spirit burner. Using chopsticks or Chinese wire strainers, cook chicken and vegetables in the stock then dip in the dipping sauce to eat. When this is completed, add noodles and Chinese leaves, and ladle noodle soup into warmed bowls.

Serves 6-8

PUMPKIN FONDUE

4 small pumpkins or squash, the size of a grapefruit
10oz creamy blue cheese such as Dolcelatte
1 cup heavy cream
4 tablespoons fresh white bread crumbs
2 teaspoons chopped fresh sage
salt and freshly ground black pepper
HERB BREADSTICKS
1lb package ciabatta bread mix
1 tablespoon dried oregano
1 tablespoon caraway seeds
oil, for brushing
flour, for dusting

Preheat the oven to 450F (230C). To make breadsticks, follow package instructions to after first rising of dough.

Turn dough on to a floured board, add oregano and caraway seeds, and knead again. Roll out to approximately ¼ inch thickness and slice into ¾ inch lengths. Brush a baking sheet with oil. Arrange breadsticks on baking sheet and leave in a warm place for about 10 minutes to rise. Dust with flour and bake for 15 minutes or until browned. Leave to cool and set aside. Reduce the oven temperature to 375F (190C). Slice the tops off pumpkins and scoop out the seeds and fibers.

Crumble half the cheese into pumpkins; top with half the cream. Scatter 1 tablespoon of bread crumbs in each pumpkin then top with remaining cheese and cream. Scatter sage over and season with salt and pepper. Replace tops on pumpkins then place in an ovenproof dish. Bake for 45 minutes or until cheese is bubbling and pumpkins are soft. Serve with breadsticks to dip in then scrape out pumpkin flesh with a spoon.

Serves 4

— CHEESE & TOMATO FONDUE —

2 cups canned tomato purée
scant 1 cup cream cheese
sugar, to taste
few drops Tabasco sauce
salt and freshly ground black pepper
frankfurters and cubes of ham, to serve
CORNMEAL MUFFINS
½ cup self rising flour
1½ teaspoons baking powder
salt and freshly ground black pepper
1 cup fine cornmeal
½ cup grated Cheddar cheese
2 tablespoons butter, melted
1 extra large egg, beaten
⅔ cup milk

Preheat the oven to 400F (200C). Line
12 mini muffin pans with paper mini muffin
cases. To make the muffins, sift flour, baking
powder, salt, and pepper into a bowl then
stir in cornmeal and cheese. (See above.) In
a bowl, mix together butter, egg, and milk.
Pour on to the dry ingredients and mix
quickly until just combined. Do not
overmix. Spoon the batter into prepared
muffin cases. Bake for 10-15 minutes until
well risen and golden brown. Leave to cool.
Arrange on serving plates with the
frankfurters and ham.

Place passata and cream cheese in a fondue
pot and heat gently until cheese has melted.
Add sugar, Tabasco sauce, salt, and pepper
to taste. Heat until just below simmering
point then transfer to the fondue burner.
Serve with the corn muffins, frankfurters,
and ham for dipping.

Serves 4-6

TEMPURA

oil, for frying
1lb assorted vegetables, such as red bell pepper strips,
   eggplant and zucchini batons, scallions, mushrooms,
   snow peas, baby corn, asparagus
BATTER
1 cup all-purpose flour
1 egg, separated
1 teaspoon olive oil
salt and freshly ground black pepper
DIPPING SAUCE
2 teaspoons each sesame oil, red wine vinegar, and soy
   sauce
3 tablespoons ginger syrup (from jar of ginger)
2 tablespoons honey
4 scallions, finely sliced

To make the batter, sift flour into a bowl.
Measure 1 cup iced water into a jug and
whisk in egg yolk and olive oil. Season with
salt and pepper. Make a well in the middle
of flour and gradually whisk in liquid. (See
above.) Cover and stand for 1 hour. To
make the dipping sauce, mix together the
sesame oil, red wine vinegar, soy sauce,
ginger syrup, and honey. Transfer to small
dishes and sprinkle the scallions on top.

Whisk egg white until stiff then fold into
the batter. Heat oil in the fondue pot on top
of the stove then transfer to the lighted
spirit burner. To serve, dip vegetables into
batter, then into hot oil for 1-2 minutes
until crisp and browned. Alternatively,
spear two or three pieces of vegetables on to
skewers and cook in the hot oil. Serve with
the dipping sauce.

Serves 4

FALAFEL FONDUE

1 cup dried chickpeas, soaked overnight in cold water
  and drained
2 tablespoons chopped fresh parsley
1 tablespoon chopped fresh cilantro
1 tablespoon tahini paste
1 clove garlic, crushed
1 tablespoon lemon juice
salt and freshly ground black pepper
seasoned flour, for dusting
oil, for frying
warm pita bread, to serve
CHILI YOGURT DIP
⅔ cup Greek-style yogurt
1 fresh red chili, cored, seeded, and finely chopped
2 tablespoons chopped fresh cilantro

Process chickpeas in a blender or food
processor until as smooth as possible.
Transfer to a bowl and stir in parsley,
cilantro, tahini, garlic, lemon juice, and salt
and pepper. (See above.) Cover and set
aside for 30 minutes. To make the chili dip,
in a bowl, mix together the yogurt, chili,
cilantro, salt, and pepper. Transfer to a
serving bowl and set aside.

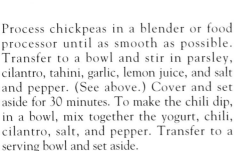

With floured hands, roll the chickpea
mixture into 1 inch balls. Dust with
seasoned flour. Arrange on serving plates.
Heat oil in the fondue pot on top of the
stove then transfer to the lighted spirit
burner. Spear the falafel on to fondue forks
and cook in the hot oil for 2 minutes or
until evenly browned. Serve with the chili
yogurt dip and warm pita bread.

Serves 4

ONION BHAJI FONDUE

4 tablespoons gram flour
½ teaspoon turmeric
½ teaspoon ground cumin
½ teaspoon ground coriander
1 teaspoon garam masala
pinch cayenne pepper
1 egg, beaten
1 large onion, quartered and very thinly sliced
1 tablespoon chopped fresh cilantro
oil, for frying
MINTED YOGURT DIP
1 cup Greek-style natural yogurt
1 clove garlic, crushed
3 tablespoons chopped fresh mint
salt and freshly ground black pepper

To make the dip, in a bowl mix together yogurt, garlic, mint, salt, and pepper. (See above.) Transfer to serving bowls and set aside. Put the gram flour, turmeric, cumin, coriander, garam masala, and cayenne pepper in a bowl and mix together. Stir in egg, season with salt and pepper, then add sliced onion and chopped cilantro. Heat the oil in the fondue pot on top of the stove then transfer to the lighted spirit burner.

To cook the bhajis, push teaspoonsful of mixture into oil with another spoon. Cook a few at a time for 2-3 minutes until crisp and golden. Remove from oil with Chinese wire nets. Serve with the yogurt dip.

Serves 4 as an appetizer

SPRING ROLLS

1 tablespoon oil
1 teaspoon sesame oil
1 clove garlic, crushed
1 fresh red chili, cored, seeded, and finely sliced
1lb pack fresh stir-fry vegetables
½ inch piece fresh root ginger, grated
1 tablespoon dry sherry or rice wine
1 tablespoon soy sauce
salt and freshly ground black pepper
12 spring roll wrappers
1 small egg, beaten
lime wedges and fresh cilantro, to garnish
oil, for frying
Dipping Sauce (see page 44), to serve

Heat oils in a wok. Add garlic and chili.

Stir-fry for 30 seconds. Add vegetables and ginger and stir-fry for 1 minute more, then drizzle sherry or rice wine and soy sauce over. Allow mixture to bubble up for 1 minute. Season with salt and pepper. Using a slotted spoon, transfer the vegetables to a dish. Set aside until cool. Soften the spring roll wrappers, following the directions on the package. Place a spoonful of filling on a wrapper.

Fold over front edge and sides and roll up neatly, sealing edges with a little beaten egg. Repeat with remaining wrappers and filling. Divide spring rolls between 4 serving plates. Garnish with lime wedges and cilantro. Heat oil in the fondue pot on top of the stove then transfer to the lighted spirit burner. Dip rolls into oil, using fondue forks or Chinese wire baskets. Cook for 2 minutes or until crisp. Serve with the dipping sauce.

Serves 4

— WILD MUSHROOM FONDUE —

¼oz dried wild mushrooms
3 tablespoons olive oil
4 shallots, finely chopped
2 cloves garlic, crushed
4oz fresh mixed wild mushrooms, chopped
3 tablespoons all-purpose flour
1 cup dry cider
12oz Emmental cheese, grated
4oz Roquefort cheese, crumbled
1 tablespoon chopped fresh tarragon
2 tablespoons light cream
TO SERVE
cubes of ham, cherry tomatoes, cooked asparagus
  spears, and cubes of bread

Place dried mushrooms in a bowl and cover with boiling water. Leave to soak for 20 minutes. Drain, reserving ½ cup of soaking liquid. Chop soaked mushrooms finely. (See above.) In the fondue pot, heat the oil. Add shallots and garlic and cook for 5 minutes until soft. Add dried and fresh mushrooms and cook for a further 4-5 minutes until soft. Stir in flour and cook for 2 minutes. Gradually stir in reserved soaking liquid, then add cider.

Cook gently, stirring, until the mixture thickens then gradually stir in Emmental and Roquefort cheeses. Add the tarragon and continue to cook gently, stirring until the cheese is melted and the mixture is smooth and creamy. Stir in cream. Transfer pot to the lighted burner and serve with the ham, vegetables, and bread to dip in.

Serves 6

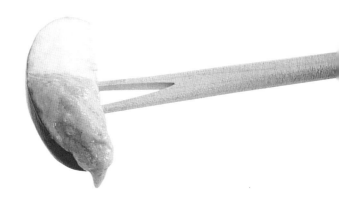

AVOCADO FONDUE

2 avocados
1 tablespoon lime juice
1 clove garlic
1 cup dry white wine
12oz Gruyère cheese, grated
1 tablespoon cornstarch
salt and freshly ground black pepper
4 tablespoons sour cream
TO SERVE
pickled jalapeño chilies, slices of apple, breadsticks,
  large peeled shrimp

Halve avocados and remove stone. Using a teaspoon, scoop out flesh and place in a bowl. Scrape out all bright green flesh next to skin.

Mash avocado until smooth then stir in lime juice. Cut garlic in half and rub round inside of the fondue pot. Pour in wine and heat until bubbling. In a bowl, toss together cheese and cornstarch then stir into the wine. Cook gently, stirring, until cheese has melted.

Add avocado and cook, stirring, until smooth and heated through. Season with salt and pepper then stir in sour cream. Transfer the pot to the lighted burner and serve with the chilies, apple, breadsticks, and shrimp for dipping.

Serves 4-6

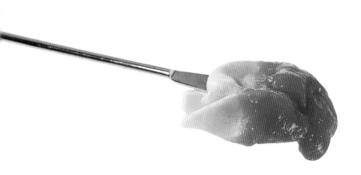

BELL PEPPER & TOMATO FONDUE

6 large tomatoes
4 red bell peppers
5 tablespoons olive oil
1 clove garlic, chopped
salt and freshly ground black pepper
1 onion, finely chopped
⅔ cup vegetable or chicken stock
2 tablespoons cornstarch, blended with a little water
fresh ravioli, cooked, to serve

Preheat the oven to 350F (190C). Oil 2 roasting pans. Cut tomatoes in half and cut red bell peppers into quarters and remove the seeds.

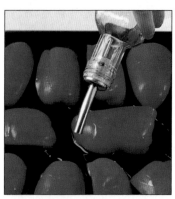

Place tomatoes, cut side up, in one of the roasting pans. Drizzle with 2 tablespoons of the olive oil and scatter with garlic. Season with salt and pepper. Place peppers in the other pan and drizzle with 2 tablespoons olive oil. Put tomatoes and peppers in the oven and roast tomatoes for 45-60 minutes until beginning to blacken round the edges. Cook the peppers, turning occasionally, until their skins are charred and blistered. Put in a plastic bag, seal and leave until cool enough to handle, then peel and chop coarsely.

Heat remaining oil in a pan. Cook onion, stirring occasionally, for 5-10 minutes, until soft. Add peppers and stock. Cover and simmer for 15 minutes. Transfer to a blender or food processor, add tomatoes, and process until smooth. Press through a sieve and pour into the fondue pot. Heat on the stove until almost simmering. Stir cornstarch into mixture. Simmer for a few minutes until thickened then transfer to the lighted fondue burner. Serve with the ravioli.

Serves 4

ASPARAGUS FONDUE

15oz canned asparagus spears
1 clove garlic, halved
1 cup dry white wine
12oz Edam cheese, grated
1 tablespoon cornstarch
4 tablespoons crème fraîche
salt and freshly ground black pepper
TO SERVE
blanched fresh asparagus spears, cooked baby
   artichoke hearts, cubes of French bread

Drain asparagus and process in a blender or
food processor until smooth. Set aside.

Rub the inside of the fondue pot with garlic,
then pour in wine and heat until bubbling.
Gradually stir in cheese and cook, stirring,
over a low heat, until cheese has melted.
Blend together cornstarch and crème
fraîche and stir into cheese mixture.
Continue to cook for a few more minutes
until thick and smooth.

Stir in asparagus purée and season with salt
and pepper. Cook for another minute until
heated through. Transfer the pot to the
lighted burner. Serve with the asparagus
spears, artichoke hearts, and bread.

Serves 4-6

CAULIFLOWER CHEESE

1 cauliflower
crisp fried onions, to garnish
CHEESE SAUCE
1 tablespoon butter
2 shallots, finely chopped
2 tablespoons all-purpose flour
1½ cups milk
½ cup grated Cheddar cheese
¼ cup grated Parmesan cheese
1 teaspoon Dijon mustard
pinch cayenne pepper
salt

Cut cauliflower into flowerets. Bring a pan of salted water to a boil.

Add cauliflower and boil for 5 minutes or until just tender. Drain thoroughly and divide between 4 serving plates. To make the cheese sauce, place butter in a saucepan and heat gently until melted. Add shallots and cook for 5 minutes until soft. Stir in flour and cook for 1 minute. Remove the pan from the heat and gradually stir in milk. Return the pan to the heat and bring to a boil then simmer gently, stirring for 2 minutes.

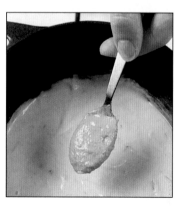

Stir in Cheddar cheese, Parmesan cheese, mustard, and cayenne pepper. Season with salt. Transfer the fondue pot to the lighted spirit burner. Scatter fried onions over the top. Spear the cauliflower flowerets on to fondue forks and dip into the sauce.

Serves 4

THAI CORN FONDUE

14oz canned corn
1¼ cups chicken stock
scant 1 cup coconut cream
1 tablespoon Thai green curry paste
1 tablespoon Thai fish sauce
2 tablespoons cornstarch
2 tablespoons chopped fresh cilantro
TO SERVE
blanched baby corn and snow peas
mini poppadoms
cooked peeled shrimp

Drain corn. In a blender or food processor, process corn to a purée and transfer to the fondue pot.

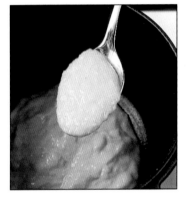

Stir in stock, coconut cream, Thai green curry paste, and fish sauce. Place over a medium heat and bring to a boil, stirring. Blend cornstarch with 2 tablespoons of cold water and add to the mixture. Bring to a boil and cook, stirring for 1 minute or until the mixture thickens.

Stir in the chopped cilantro. Transfer the pot to the lighted fondue burner and serve with the baby corn, snow peas, poppadoms, and shrimp.

Serves 4

NOTE: Vary the amount of Thai green curry sauce according to taste. For children, add a little less and for those who prefer a more fiery flavor, add more.

FONDUE SAVOYARDE

.1 clove garlic, cut in half
²/₃ cup dry white wine
1 teaspoon lemon juice
2 cups grated Gruyère cheese
2 cups grated Emmental cheese
1 tablespoon cornstarch
2 tablespoons kirsch
pinch freshly grated nutmeg
pinch cayenne pepper
TO SERVE
cubes of baguette
green salad
slices of air dried ham

Rub cut side of garlic round inside fondue pot.

Pour wine and lemon juice into the pot and place over a low heat. Heat gently until bubbling. Gradually stir in grated cheeses and heat gently, stirring, until completely melted. In a small bowl, blend together the cornstarch and kirsch, and stir into cheese mixture.

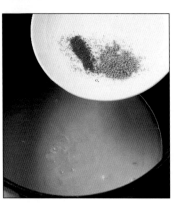

Continue to cook, stirring, for 2-3 minutes until mixture is thick and creamy. Add nutmeg and cayenne pepper. Transfer pot to the lighted spirit burner. To serve, spear cubes of bread on to the fondue forks and dip into cheese mixture. Serve with the salad and air dried ham.

Serves 4-6

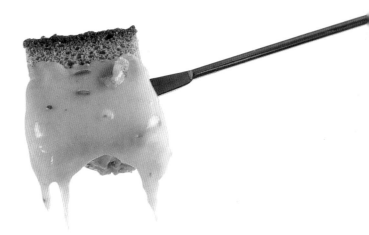

GOUDA CHEESE FONDUE

½ small onion
2 teaspoons cumin seeds
⅔ cup dry white wine
1 teaspoon lemon juice
3½ cups grated Gouda cheese
2 teaspoons cornstarch
2 tablespoons gin
freshly ground black pepper
pinch nutmeg
light rye bread cubes, to serve

Rub inside of the fondue pot with cut side of onion. Place cumin seeds in pot and heat gently for 1 minute.

Add wine and lemon juice. Heat until nearly boiling and then add grated cheese. Heat gently, stirring, until cheese melts. In a small bowl, blend together cornstarch and gin. Stir into cheese mixture.

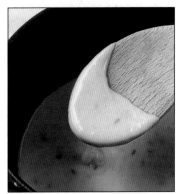

As soon as fondue thickens and comes just to a simmer, take off the heat. Season with pepper and nutmeg. Place the fondue pot over the lighted spirit burner and serve with the rye bread.

Serves 4

FONDUE INDIENNE

1 clove garlic, halved
3 cups grated Cheddar cheese
2 tablespoons all-purpose flour
1 small onion, grated
1½ cups dry white wine
2 teaspoons curry paste
2 tablespoons mango chutney
salt and freshly ground black pepper
cayenne pepper, to garnish
naan bread, to serve

Rub the inside of the fondue pot with the cut clove of garlic. Crush the garlic.

Place cheese and flour in a plastic bag and toss to combine. Place crushed garlic, onion, wine, and curry paste in the fondue pot and bring almost to a simmer. Gradually stir in cheese, allowing it to melt between each addition.

Stir in mango chutney, and salt and pepper to taste. Place on the lighted spirit burner. Sprinkle a little cayenne pepper over. Serve with pieces of naan bread.

Serves 4

NOTE: If the mango chutney has large pieces of fruit in it, chop it finely.

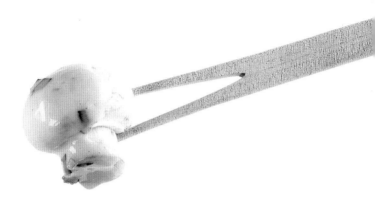

FRENCH BRIE FONDUE

13oz ripe French Brie
¼ cup butter
1 onion, finely chopped
1 clove garlic, crushed
¼ cup all-purpose flour
1¼ cups chicken or vegetable stock
⅔ cup heavy cream
1 tablespoon chopped fresh tarragon
salt and freshly ground black pepper
TO SERVE
grapes
cubes of French bread
raw button mushrooms

Cut away rind from Brie and slice cheese thinly. Set aside.

Melt butter in the fondue pot over a low heat. Add onion and garlic, and cook gently for 10 minutes until softened. Sprinkle flour over and cook for 1-2 minutes, stirring. Gradually add stock and continue to stir until mixture thickens. Simmer gently for 2-3 minutes.

Stir sliced Brie and cream into the fondue. Cook, stirring, until cheese has melted and mixture is smooth. Stir in tarragon, and season with salt and pepper. Transfer the fondue pot to the lighted spirit burner. To serve, spear grapes, bread, and mushrooms on to skewers or fondue forks and dip into the fondue.

Serves 4-6

- SMOKY CHEESE & HAM FONDUE -

1 cup grated Gruyère cheese
2 cups grated smoked Cheddar cheese
1 tablespoon cornstarch
1 tablespoon butter
1 small onion, finely chopped
1 clove garlic, crushed
²⁄₃ cup dry white wine
½ teaspoon smoked paprika
4oz smoked ham, chopped
TO SERVE
wedges of apple
cubes of crusty bread

In a bowl, toss together the grated cheese
and the cornstarch.

In a saucepan, melt butter over a low heat.
Add onion and garlic and cook gently for
10 minutes until softened. Place wine in the
fondue pot and heat gently until bubbling.
Gradually stir in grated cheeses and heat
gently, stirring, until completely melted.

Stir in onion and garlic, then paprika and
ham, and cook for a few more minutes until
thick and smooth. Transfer the fondue pot
to the lighted spirit burner. To serve, spear
apple and bread on to skewers or fondue
forks and dip into the fondue.

Serves 4

SOMERSET FONDUE

½ small onion
1¼ cups dry hard cider
1 teaspoon lemon juice
4 cups grated farmhouse Cheddar cheese
1 tablespoon cornstarch
2 tablespoons dry sherry
pinch mustard powder
1 teaspoon Worcestershire sauce
1 teaspoon chopped fresh sage
salt and freshly ground black pepper
TO SERVE
cubes of crusty farmhouse bread
wedges of apple
celery sticks
pickle

Rub inside of the fondue pot with cut side of onion. Place cider and lemon juice in fondue pot and heat gently until bubbling. Gradually stir in grated cheese and heat gently, stirring, until completely melted. In a small bowl, blend together cornstarch and sherry. Add mustard and Worcestershire sauce. Stir into cheese mixture.

Continue to cook, stirring until thick and smooth. Stir in sage, and season with salt and pepper. Transfer the fondue pot to the lighted spirit burner. To serve, spear bread on to fondue forks to dip into fondue and serve accompanied by apple, celery, and pickle.

Serves 6

ITALIAN PESTO FONDUE

1 clove garlic
scant 1 cup Soave wine
2 cups grated Gruyère cheese
1½ cups dolcelatte cheese, cubed
½ cup grated Parmesan cheese
1 tablespoon cornstarch
2 tablespoons milk
1 tablespoon pesto sauce
salt and freshly ground black pepper
TO SERVE
foccacia and ciabatta bread cut into cubes
slices of salami
olives

Cut clove of garlic in half and rub cut side round the inside of the fondue pot. (See above.) Place wine in the fondue pot and heat gently until bubbling. Gradually stir in prepared cheeses and heat gently, stirring, until completely melted. In a small bowl, blend together the cornstarch and milk. Stir into the cheese mixture. Continue to cook, stirring, until thick and smooth.

Stir in pesto, and season with salt and pepper. Transfer the fondue pot to the lighted spirit burner. To serve, spear bread and salami on to fondue forks to dip into the fondue, and serve accompanied by the olives.

Serves 6

VARIATION: Instead of bread and salami, serve cooked tortelloni to dip into the fondue.

—— WELSH RAREBIT FONDUE ——

1 tablespoon butter
1 small onion, finely chopped
1½ cups light ale
2 cups grated Caerphilly cheese
1 cup grated Welsh Cheddar cheese
1 tablespoon cornstarch
2 tablespoons milk
1 teaspoon Dijon mustard
1 teaspoon Worcestershire sauce
pinch cayenne pepper
salt and freshly ground black pepper
thick slices of toast, cut into cubes, to serve

Place butter in the fondue pot and melt over a low heat.

Add onion, and cook gently for 10 minutes until softened. Add light ale, and heat gently until bubbling. Gradually stir in grated cheeses, and heat gently, stirring, until completely melted. In a small bowl, mix together the cornstarch and milk. Stir into cheese mixture.

Continue to cook, stirring, until thick and smooth. Stir in mustard, Worcestershire sauce, and cayenne pepper. Season with salt and pepper. Transfer the fondue pot to the lighted spirit burner. To serve, spear cubes of toasted bread on fondue forks and dip into fondue.

Serves 4-6

——— MEXICAN CHILI FONDUE ———

4 cups grated Monterey Jack cheese
2 tablespoons cornstarch
1 clove garlic
generous 1 cup Mexican lager
1 tablespoon lime juice
1-2 fresh red chilies, cored, seeded and finely chopped
salt and freshly ground black pepper
1 tablespoon chopped fresh cilantro
FRIED SHALLOTS
8 shallots, thinly sliced
4 tablespoons vegetable oil
TO SERVE
pickled jalapeño chilies
tomato wedges
cubes of avocado
warm flour tortillas

Make the fried shallots. Heat oil in a skillet, add shallots, and cook, stirring, for 5 minutes or until browned. (See above.) Drain on kitchen paper and set aside. In a bowl, toss together the grated cheese and the cornstarch. Cut clove of garlic in half and rub cut side round inside of the fondue pot. Add lager, lime juice, and chilies, and heat gently until bubbling.

Gradually stir in grated cheese and cook gently, stirring, until completely melted. Season with salt and pepper. Stir in chopped cilantro and fried shallots. Transfer the fondue pot to the lighted spirit burner. Cut tortillas into strips, roll up, and spear on to fondue forks to dip into the fondue, with the jalapeño chilies, tomato, and avocado.

Serves 4-6

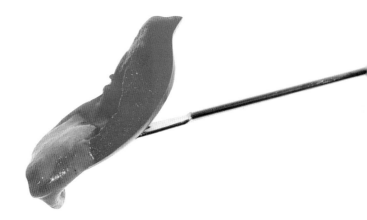

SPANISH FONDUE

1 clove garlic
generous 1 cup dry Spanish white wine
2 cups grated Gruyère cheese
2 cups grated Manchego cheese
1 tablespoon cornstarch
2 tablespoons dry sherry
2 teaspoons smoked Spanish paprika
salt and freshly ground black pepper
TO SERVE
chunks of chorizo sausage
pieces of red bell pepper
cubes of crusty country bread
olives
cubes of membrillo (quince paste)

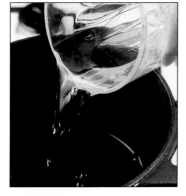

Cut clove of garlic in half and rub the cut side round inside of the fondue pot. Place wine in the fondue pot and heat gently until bubbling. (See above.) Gradually stir in the prepared cheeses and heat gently, stirring, until completely melted. In a small bowl, blend together cornstarch and sherry. Stir into the cheese mixture. Continue to cook, stirring, until thick and smooth.

Stir in paprika and season with salt and pepper. Transfer the fondue pot to the lighted spirit burner. To serve, spear chorizo sausage, bell pepper, and bread on to fondue forks to dip into the fondue; serve accompanied by olives and membrillo.

Serves 4-6

CREAMY HERB & GARLIC FONDUE

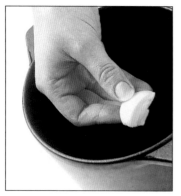

1 clove garlic
⅔ cup dry white wine
1 tablespoon cornstarch
1¼ cups crème fraîche
1¼ cups full-fat soft cheese with garlic and herbs
pinch freshly grated nutmeg
salt and freshly ground black pepper
1 tablespoon chopped fresh chives
TO SERVE
cubes of French bread
cherry tomatoes
button mushrooms

Cut clove of garlic in half and rub the cut side round the inside of the fondue pot.

Pour ½ cup of the wine into the fondue pot and heat gently until bubbling. In a small bowl, blend cornstarch with the remaining wine. Add to the fondue pot and cook, stirring, until thickened. Reduce the heat and add crème fraîche and soft cheese. Stir until cheese has melted.

Add nutmeg and season with salt and pepper. Sprinkle with chopped chives, and transfer the fondue pot to the lighted spirit burner. To serve, spear bread, tomatoes, and mushrooms on to fondue forks and dip into the fondue.

Serves 4-6

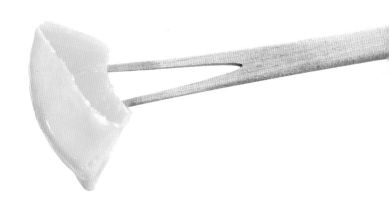

— CHILDRENS' PARTY FONDUE —

2 tablespoons butter
¼ cup all-purpose flour
2 cups milk
½ cup cream cheese
1½ cups grated Edam cheese
½ cup heavy cream
½ teaspoon dry mustard
salt and freshly ground black pepper
TO SERVE
carrot and celery sticks
cherry tomatoes
scallions
wedges of apple
pineapple cubes
cooked baby potatoes

Arrange vegetables and fruit on individual serving plates. Place butter in the fondue pot and heat until melted. (See above.) Stir in flour and cook, stirring, for 1 minute. Gradually stir in milk, then bring to a boil and cook, stirring, until thickened and smooth. Stir in cream cheese, Edam cheese, and cream. Heat gently, stirring, until cheese has melted and mixture is smooth.

Stir in mustard, and season with salt and pepper. Transfer the fondue pot to the lighted spirit burner. To serve, spear vegetables and fruit on to fondue forks and dip into the fondue.

Serves 5-6

ALPINE TARTIFLETTE

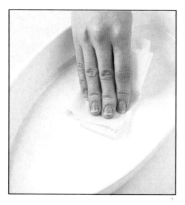

butter, for greasing
12oz potatoes, scrubbed
2 tablespoons butter
1 small onion, chopped
4oz smoked bacon, cut into small pieces
1 Reblochon cheese
salt and freshly ground black pepper
5 tablespoons light cream
green salad, to serve

Preheat the oven to 425F (220C). Butter a gratin dish. Place scrubbed potatoes in a pan of cold water and bring to a boil.

Cook for 15-20 minutes until tender. Drain, and when cool enough to handle, peel, and cut into thick slices. Meanwhile, heat butter in a skillet. Add onion and cook for a few minutes until soft. Add bacon and cook until lightly browned. Remove onion and bacon with a slotted spoon, drain on paper towels, and set aside. Add potato slices to the pan and cook for 2-3 minutes on each side, until golden.

Cut the Reblochon in half and then into cubes, leaving the crust on. Make layers of potato, bacon, onion, and cheese, seasoning each layer with salt and pepper. Pour cream over the top, and cook in the oven for 10-12 minutes or until the top has browned. Serve with green salad.

Serves 2

RACLETTE

2lb small new potatoes
salt and freshly ground black pepper
1lb Raclette cheese
TO SERVE
air dried ham
salami
pickled gherkins

Scrub potatoes and place in a pan of cold salted water. Bring to a boil and cook for 10-15 minutes until tender. Drain and place in a warm serving bowl. Season with salt and pepper.

To cook the cheese, slice cheese thinly and place a layer of slices on a shallow metal tray and place under a hot broiler until it starts to melt. Scrape the top melted layer of cheese off with a palette knife.

Place melted cheese on top of potatoes. Continue to cook the remaining cheese in the same way. Serve with the ham, salami, and gherkins.

Serves 4

—— CHEESE FONDUE TARTS ——

15oz puff pastry
1¼ cups grated Beaufort cheese
1¼ cups grated Jarlsberg cheese
1 clove garlic, crushed
⅔ cup light cream
1 tablespoon lemon juice
2 teaspoons cornstarch
3 tablespoons vodka
salt and freshly ground black pepper
2 tablespoons chopped fresh chives

Preheat the oven to 425F (220C). On a floured surface, roll the pastry out to ⅛ inch thick and cut out twelve 4 inch circles.

Place circles in a 12-cup muffin pan. Prick bottoms and chill for 10 minutes. Press foil into pastry cases and fill with dried beans. Bake for 15-20 minutes then remove foil and beans and bake for 5 more minutes until golden.

Meanwhile, put grated cheeses, garlic, cream, and lemon juice in a pan. Cook over a gentle heat, stirring, until smooth. In a small bowl combine cornstarch and vodka, add to cheese mixture, and cook for 2 minutes. Season with salt and pepper, and stir in chives. Divide cheese fondue between the pastry cases and serve at once.

Makes 12

BAKED CAMEMBERT

1 small whole Camembert cheese in its box
2 cloves garlic
2 tablespoons dry white wine (optional)
chunks of crusty bread, to serve
BACON-WRAPPED POTATOES
16 small new potatoes, total weight about 1lb
salt
8 slices bacon
1 teaspoon Dijon mustard

Preheat the oven to 400F (200C). Prepare potatoes. Scrub them and place in a pan of salted water. Bring to a boil and boil for 10-15 minutes until tender. Drain.

Meanwhile, remove wrapping around cheese. Peel garlic cloves and cut into slivers. Push garlic slivers into the surface of cheese. Drizzle wine over, if using, so that it soaks into the holes. Remove cheese from box and wrap in foil. Bake the cheese in the oven for 25-30 minutes until bubbling.

Cut each bacon slice in half across. Stretch out slightly with the back of a knife and smear with a little mustard. Wrap a piece of bacon round each potato, and secure with a wooden toothpick. Broil potatoes, turning once, until bacon is brown and crisp. Remove foil from the cheese and serve in the box, with bacon-wrapped potatoes and crusty bread.

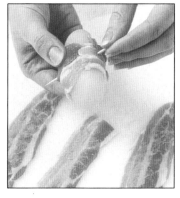

Serves 2-3

– CLASSIC CHOCOLATE FONDUE –

9oz dark chocolate
⅔ cup heavy cream
2 tablespoons brandy
selection of fruit such as strawberries, pineapple,
  banana, ground cherries, figs, and kiwi fruit, to
  serve
LADYFINGERS
1½oz superfine sugar
1 egg
½ cup all-purpose flour, sifted

Preheat the oven to 375C (190C) Line a
baking sheet with non-stick parchment. To
make ladyfingers, place superfine sugar and
egg in a large bowl.

Set bowl over a pan of barely simmering
water and whisk together until thick and
mousse-like. (See above.) Remove bowl
from heat and gently fold in flour. Using a
pastry bag fitted with a ½ inch plain tube,
pipe finger lengths of mixture on to the
prepared baking sheet. Bake for 6-8 minutes
until golden. Transfer ladyfingers to a wire
rack to cool.

Break up chocolate and place in the fondue
pot with cream and brandy. Heat gently,
stirring, until chocolate has melted and
mixture is smooth. Transfer fondue pot to
the lighted spirit burner and serve with the
ladyfingers and fruit.

Serves 4-6

VARIATION: For children, substitute orange
juice for brandy.

BLACK FOREST FONDUE

14oz can pitted black cherries
²/₃ cup heavy cream
1 tablespoon kirsch
1 tablespoon cornstarch
CHOCOLATE CAKE
2 eggs
½ cup softened butter
½ cup superfine sugar
1 cup self rising flour
½ teaspoon baking powder
2 tablespoons cocoa
1 tablespoon milk

Preheat the oven to 375F (190C). Grease an 8-inch shallow, square pan.

To make the chocolate cake, put eggs, butter, and sugar into a bowl. (See above.) Sift flour, baking powder, and cocoa over. Add milk and beat together until smooth. Turn mixture into prepared pan and bake for 25 minutes until cooked and firm to the touch. Turn on to a wire rack and leave to cool. Cut into small squares when cold.

Empty cherries and their juice into a blender or food processor, and process until reasonably smooth. Transfer to a fondue pot, stir in cream, and heat until simmering. Add kirsch. In a small bowl, blend together cornstarch and 1 tablespoon of water. Add to the fondue pot and continue to cook, stirring, until the mixture thickens. Transfer the fondue pot to the lighted spirit burner. Serve with the chocolate cake to dip in.

Serves 4

STRAWBERRY & CREAM FONDUE

½ cup strawberries
confectioners' sugar
13oz white chocolate
1 cup heavy cream
2 tablespoons framboise or kirsch
fresh strawberries, to serve

Place strawberries in a blender or food processor and process until smooth. Press through a sieve into a bowl. Add confectioners' sugar to taste.

Roughly chop or break up chocolate into pieces and place in the fondue pot. Add the heavy cream. Over a low heat, heat gently, stirring continuously, until chocolate melts. Add the framboise or kirsch, and stir until smooth.

Place the fondue pot over a lighted spirit burner to keep warm. Swirl the strawberry purée on the surface of the cream sauce. Serve with fresh strawberries.

Serves 6

CARIBBEAN CHOCOLATE FONDUE

1 pineapple
1 mango
2 bananas
juice ½ lime
13oz good-quality dark chocolate
scant 1 cup cream of coconut
2 tablespoons white rum
½ teaspoon freshly grated nutmeg

Cut the leafy top and the bottom off pineapple. Cut away skin and cut pineapple into quarters, lengthwise. Cut out core and cut each quarter into cubes.

Peel mango then cut down on either side of pit to remove flesh. Cut into cubes. Cut bananas into slices and sprinkle with lime juice.

Break up chocolate into a fondue pot. Add cream of coconut and heat gently on the stove, stirring, until chocolate melts. Stir in rum and nutmeg, then place over a lighted spirit burner to keep warm. Serve with the fruit.

Serves 6

-FRUITS OF THE FOREST FONDUE-

1lb 2oz package of frozen fruits of the forest or
summer fruits
4 tablespoons confectioners' sugar
2 tablespoons crème de cassis or kirsch
2 tablespoons cornstarch
scant 1 cup fromage frais
MINI LEMON CAKES
2 eggs
½ cup softened butter
½ cup superfine sugar
1 cup self rising flour
grated rind 1 lemon
1 tablespoon lemon juice

Preheat the oven to 375F (190C). Arrange
40 paper petit-four cases on a baking sheet.
(See above.) To make lemon cakes, put
eggs, butter, and sugar into a bowl. Sift flour
over. Add lemon rind and juice, and beat
together until smooth. Put a teaspoon of
mixture in each of the petit-four cases and
bake for 10-15 minutes until cooked and
firm to the touch. Leave to cool on a wire
rack before removing from the paper cases.

Process fruit and any juice in a blender or
food processor, then press through a sieve
into a fondue pot. Stir in confectioners'
sugar; heat gently on the stove until almost
simmering. Blend together crème de cassis or
kirsch and cornstarch and stir into fruit
purée. Cook, stirring, for 2-3 minutes until
thickened. Stir in fromage frais and heat
gently, stirring, until well blended. Transfer
the fondue pot to the lighted spirit burner
and serve with lemon cakes for dipping.

Serves 6

BUTTERSCOTCH FONDUE

¼ cup unsalted butter
¾ cup soft brown sugar
2 tablespoons golden syrup or corn syrup
½ teaspoon grated lemon rind
1 teaspoon lemon juice
2 tablespoons cornstarch
14oz can evaporated milk
fresh fruit, to serve
VANILLA COOKIES
1 vanilla bean
½ cup unsalted butter
⅓ cup superfine sugar
1 egg yolk
1 cup self rising flour

To make the cookies, slit vanilla bean
lengthwise and scrape black seeds into a
large bowl. (See above.) Add butter and
sugar, and beat together until light and
fluffy. Beat in egg yolk, then stir in flour to
make a stiff dough. Wrap dough in plastic
wrap and chill for 15 minutes. Preheat the
oven to 375F (190C). Grease 2 or 3 baking
sheets. Divide dough into 30 small balls and
place well apart on baking sheets. Flatten
slightly. Bake for 15 minutes until golden
brown. Transfer to wire racks to cool.

To make fondue, place butter, sugar, syrup,
and lemon rind and juice in a fondue pot
and heat gently until sugar has dissolved.
Boil for 1 minute. Blend cornstarch and
2 tablespoons of the evaporated milk. Stir
remaining evaporated milk into sugar
mixture. Heat until just simmering then
simmer for 2-3 minutes. Stir in blended
cornstarch then bring to a boil, stirring, until
smooth and thick. Transfer to the lighted
burner and serve with cookies and fruit.

Serves 6

BANOFFEE FONDUE

9oz vanilla fudge
1¼ cup heavy cream
sliced bananas, to serve
MINI CHOCOLATE MUFFINS
1½oz dark chocolate
1¼ cups all-purpose flour
1½ teaspoons baking powder
pinch salt
½ teaspoon ground cinnamon
¼ cup superfine sugar
1 egg
½ cup milk
¼ cup butter, melted and cooled slightly

Preheat the oven to 400F (200C).

Arrange 20 petit-four cases on a baking sheet. To make the muffins, chop the chocolate into small pieces. Sift the flour, baking powder, salt and cinnamon into a bowl. In another bowl, whisk together the sugar, egg, milk and melted butter. Add the dry ingredients and the chocolate and fold together quickly and lightly until just combined. Divide the mixture between the petit-four cases and bake in the oven for 15 minutes or until well risen and golden. Transfer to a wire rack to cool.

To make the fondue, place the fudge and cream in the fondue pot and heat gently, stirring until melted and smooth. Transfer the fondue pot to the lighted burner. To serve, spear the banana and muffin cakes on to bamboo skewers or fondue forks.

Serves 6

—— SPICED APRICOT FONDUE ——

2 x 14oz cans apricot halves in natural juice
1 sachet wine mulling spices or 1 tablespoon mulling
  spices tied in muslin
2 tablespoons cornstarch
1¼ cups fromage frais
kiwi fruit, to serve
ALMOND MACAROONS
2 extra large egg whites
¼ cup ground almonds
½ cup superfine sugar
1 tablespoon cornstarch
few drops almond extract
24 split blanched almonds

Preheat the oven to 375F (190C).

Line 2 or 3 baking sheets with non-stick paper. Make the macaroons. Reserve 2 teaspoons of egg white for brushing. In a large bowl, whisk remaining egg whites until frothy. Stir in almonds, sugar, cornstarch, and almond extract. Mix together well. Place 24 small spoonfuls of mixture on to baking sheets. Smooth out slightly with the back of a spoon. Place a split blanched almond in center of each macaroon and brush the top with reserved egg white. Bake for 10-15 minutes until a pale golden brown. Leave for 5 minutes then cool on a wire rack.

Place apricots and juice in fondue pot with spice sachet. Heat until simmering then remove from heat and leave to cool. Remove sachet, and place apricots and juice in a blender or food processor. Process to a purée and return to fondue pot. Reheat gently. In a small bowl, blend cornstarch with a little water. Add to apricot purée and continue to heat, stirring, until thickened. Stir in fromage frais then transfer fondue pot to lighted burner. Serve with kiwi fruit and macaroons.

Serves 4-6

— LEMON MERINGUE FONDUE —

4 tablespoons cornstarch
1 ¼ cups coconut milk
grated rind and juice 2 lemons
¼ cup superfine sugar
pieces of mango, to serve
MERINGUES
2 egg whites
½ cup superfine sugar
½ teaspoon vanilla extract

Preheat the oven to 225F (110C). Line 2 or 3 baking sheets with non-stick paper. Put egg whites in a large clean bowl and whisk until meringue holds soft peaks.

Add sugar, 1 tablespoonful at a time, whisking well after each addition. Continue whisking until stiff and glossy. Fold in vanilla with a rubber spatula. Put 24 teaspoonfuls of mixture on to lined baking sheets. Bake for 1-1½ hours until dry and crisp. Turn off oven and leave meringues in oven to cool. Remove from the paper when cool.

To make the fondue, put cornstarch and a little of the coconut milk in the fondue pot and stir to make a paste. Stir in remaining coconut milk. Bring to a boil on top of the stove, stirring, and continue to cook for 2-3 minutes until thickened. Remove from heat, and add lemon rind and juice, and sugar. Reheat then transfer the fondue pot to the lighted spirit burner. Serve with the mango and meringues.

Serves 4-6

TIRAMISU FONDUE

generous 1 cup mascarpone cheese
2 tablespoons rum
3½oz dark chocolate
1 tablespoon instant coffee granules
1 tablespoon superfine sugar (optional)
TO SERVE
squares of panettone
Italian ladyfingers
strawberries

Place mascarpone cheese in the fondue pot
with the rum. Heat gently on top of the
stove, stirring, until mascarpone melts.

Break up chocolate into small pieces and
add to the fondue pot. Continue to heat
gently until chocolate melts.

Add coffee granules and stir until mixture is
smooth. Taste the fondue and add sugar if
desired. Transfer the fondue pot to the
lighted spirit burner and serve with
panettone, ladyfingers, and strawberries.

Serves 4

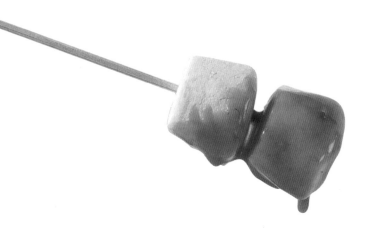

MARSHMALLOW FONDUE

8oz marshmallows
⅔ cup bottled raspberry or strawberry sauce
⅔ cup heavy cream
1-2 tablespoons lemon juice (optional)
TO SERVE
marshmallows
ladyfingers
strawberries

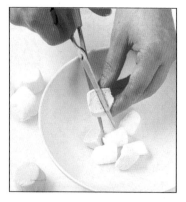

Using wet scissors, snip marshmallows into pieces and place in the fondue pot.

Add fruit sauce and cream. Place over a very low heat and cook gently, stirring, until marshmallows have melted and mixture is smooth.

Add lemon juice, to taste, if desired. Transfer the fondue pot to the lighted spirit burner and serve with marshmallows, ladyfingers, and strawberries.

Serves 4

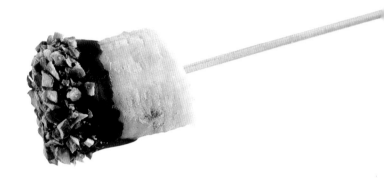

- BANANA & CHOCOLATE BITES -

6 firm ripe bananas
¼ cup shelled pistachio nuts
8oz dark chocolate
4 tablespoons light cream

Peel bananas and cut them into 1 inch lengths. Cover a metal baking sheet with plastic wrap.

Arrange banana slices in a single layer on the baking sheet and place in the freezer. Leave in the freezer for at least 3 hours or until completely frozen. Coarsely chop pistachio nuts and divide between 4 small shallow dishes. When ready to serve, break up chocolate into the fondue pot. Add cream and heat gently on top of the stove, stirring, until chocolate is melted and mixture is smooth.

Transfer fondue pot to the lighted spirit burner. Bring banana pieces to the table on the metal baking sheet. To serve, spear the banana on to bamboo skewers or fondue forks, dip into the chocolate, and then into the chopped nuts.

Serves 6

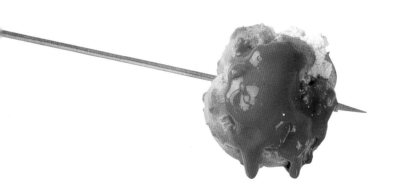

– CHOCOLATE ORANGE FONDUE –

12oz dark chocolate chips
4 tablespoons heavy cream
¼ cup orange juice
1 teaspoon grated orange rind
PROFITEROLES
¼ cup butter
2½oz all-purpose flour, sifted
2 eggs, lightly beaten
⅔ cup heavy cream, whipped

Preheat the oven to 425F (220C). Butter 2 baking sheets. Make the profiteroles. Place butter in a pan with ⅔ cup water. Bring just to a boil and remove from the heat.

Add flour to pan, stirring constantly with a wooden spoon, until combined. (See above.) Return pan to heat and continue beating over a low heat until mixture is smooth and pulls away from sides of the pan. Remove from heat and leave to cool for a minute. Beat in eggs, a little at a time, until mixture is smooth and glossy. Using 2 spoons, place 24 walnut-size mounds of mixture well apart on the baking sheets. Bake for 20 minutes until well risen and golden brown. Reduce oven temperature to 350F (180C). Make a hole in each bun.

Return buns to the oven for 5 minutes. Cool on a wire rack. Spoon a little cream into each bun. Place chocolate chips, cream, and orange juice in a large microwave-safe bowl. Cover and microwave at full power for 1 minute. Stir until smooth. Heat for a few more seconds, if necessary, until all the chocolate is melted. Stir in orange rind. Transfer to a fondue pot and place on a lighted burner. Spear profiteroles on to bamboo skewers or fondue forks, to serve.

Serves 4-6

CAPPUCINO FONDUE

8oz white chocolate
¼ cup strong espresso coffee
⅔ cup heavy cream
drinking chocolate, for sprinkling
PISTACHIO BISCOTTI
2 cups all-purpose flour
1 teaspoon baking powder
pinch salt
¼ cup superfine sugar
2 eggs
grated rind 1 lemon
1 tablespoon lemon juice
¼ cup blanched almonds, toasted and roughly
  chopped
⅓ cup shelled pistachio nuts, roughly chopped

Preheat the oven to 350F (180C). Line a baking sheet with non-stick parchment. To make biscotti, sift flour, baking powder, and salt into a mixing bowl. Stir in sugar, eggs, lemon rind and juice, and nuts. Mix together to form a firm dough. (See above.) Roll dough into a ball, cut in half, and roll each portion into a roll about 1¼ inches in diameter. Place rolls on the baking sheet at least 3½ inches apart. Lightly flatten rolls and bake for 15-20 minutes until golden brown. Remove from oven and leave to cool and firm up for 5 minutes.

With a serrated knife, cut biscotti at an angle into ½ inch thick slices. Arrange slices on baking sheet and return to the oven for a further 15 minutes, turning once. Transfer to a wire rack to cool. To make the fondue, place chocolate, coffee, and cream in the fondue pot and heat gently on top of the stove until chocolate has melted and mixture is smooth. Sprinkle with drinking chocolate then transfer to the lighted spirit burner and serve with the biscotti.

Serves 4

- CHOCOLATE & HONEY FONDUE -

10oz dark chocolate
1 generous tablespoon honey
1¼ cups heavy cream
SPICED FRUIT
14oz ready-to-eat dried fruit such as apricots
    and prunes
1 cinnamon stick
1 star anise
4 cloves
1 tablespoon honey

To prepare the fruit, place in a saucepan and cover with water. Add cinnamon stick, star anise, and cloves, and bring to a boil.

Stir in honey and remove from the heat. Set aside and leave until cold. Drain fruit and pat dry on paper towels. Arrange on 6 individual plates.

Break up the chocolate and place in the fondue pot with honey and cream. Heat gently, stirring, until chocolate has melted and mixture is smooth. Transfer the fondue pot to the lighted spirit burner and serve with the fruit.

Serves 6

NOTE: For both the fondue and fruit, choose a fragrant blossom honey such as Mexican wildflower honey.

– RHUBARB & CUSTARD FONDUE –

1¼lb cans rhubarb in syrup
2 cups fresh custard
GINGER SPONGE
2 eggs
½ cup softened butter
½ cup golden superfine sugar
1 cup self rising flour
1 teaspoon ground ginger
pinch baking powder
2 pieces ginger from a jar of stem ginger in syrup,
  finely chopped
1 tablespoon syrup from the ginger jar

Preheat oven to 350F (180C). Grease an
8-inch shallow, square cake pan.

To make the ginger sponge, put eggs, butter,
and superfine sugar in a bowl. Sift flour,
ginger, and baking powder into the bowl.
Add chopped ginger and syrup, and beat
together until thoroughly blended. (See
above.) Turn the mixture into the prepared
pan and bake for 25 minutes or until golden
and firm to the touch. Leave in the pan for
5 minutes then turn out on to a wire rack to
cool. Cut into small squares when cold.

To make the fondue, drain rhubarb and
place in a blender or food processor. Process
to a purée then place in the fondue pot with
the custard. Heat on top of the stove until
hot but not boiling. Transfer the fondue pot
to the lighted spirit burner and serve with
the ginger sponge.

Serves 4-6

ROUILLE

2 slices white bread, crusts removed
2 red bell peppers, seeded and quartered
2 fresh red chilies, cored, seeded, and chopped
2 cloves garlic, crushed
olive oil

Place bread in a shallow dish with 3-4 tablespoons cold water and soak for 10 minutes.

Grill red bell pepper quarters, skin side up, until the skin is charred and blistered. Place in a plastic bag until cool enough to handle. Peel off skins and chop flesh roughly.

Place red bell pepper flesh in a blender or food processor. Drain the bread and squeeze out the excess moisture. Add to bell peppers with chilies and garlic. Process to a coarse paste then gradually add enough olive oil to give the desired consistency. Transfer to small serving bowls.

Serves 4-6

CHILI TOMATO SAUCE

1 onion
2 stalks celery
1 clove garlic
1 red bell pepper
1 red chili
2 tablespoons oil
14oz canned chopped tomatoes
1 teaspoon molasses or dark soft brown sugar
salt and freshly ground black pepper
chopped fresh cilantro, to garnish

Finely chop the onion and celery stalks. Crush garlic and seed red bell pepper and chop. Core and seed the chili and chop very finely.

Heat oil in a saucepan. Add onion, celery, garlic, and red bell pepper, and cook for 10 minutes until soft. Add chili, tomatoes, and molasses, and season with salt and pepper.

Bring to a boil, cover, and simmer gently for 20-30 minutes until thickened and well blended. Garnish with chopped cilantro.

Serves 4-6

TWO MAYONNAISES

SAFFRON MAYONNAISE:
⅔ cup fish stock
½ teaspoon saffron strands
⅔ cup mayonnaise
1 teaspoon lemon juice
salt and freshly ground black pepper
AIOLI:
⅔ cup mayonnaise
2 cloves garlic, crushed
1 teaspoon Dijon mustard
salt and freshly ground black pepper (optional)

To make the saffron mayonnaise, put fish stock in a saucepan and bring to a boil.

Boil until reduced to 1 tablespoon. Add saffron strands and leave to cool. Strain stock into a bowl and stir in mayonnaise. Add lemon juice and season with salt and pepper. (Salt will not be needed if the fish stock was salty.) Spoon into a serving bowl, cover and chill until required.

To make the aioli, place mayonnaise, garlic, and mustard in a bowl. Mix together and season with salt and pepper, if desired. Transfer to a serving bowl, cover and chill until required. Set aside.

Serves 4

CUMBERLAND SAUCE

1 shallot
1 orange
1 lemon
⅓ cup red currant jelly
1 teaspoon Dijon mustard
⅓ cup port
1 teaspoon arrowroot

Chop shallot very finely and place in a saucepan. With a peeler, remove the rind of orange and lemon.

Cut into very fine strips and add to the pan. Cover with cold water, bring to a boil, and cook for 5 minutes. Drain and set aside. Meanwhile, halve orange and lemon and squeeze juice. Set aside. Add red currant jelly to the pan and heat gently, stirring until melted.

Stir in mustard, port, juice of orange and lemon, blanched rind, and shallot. Cook for about 5 minutes. In a small bowl, mix arrowroot to a paste with a 1 tablespoon of cold water. Add to the sauce in the pan. Simmer for a further 2-3 minutes until slightly thickened then leave to cool before serving.

Serves 4

TOMATO & OLIVE SALSA

4 plum tomatoes
1¼ cups mixed pitted green and black olives, roughly
   chopped
1 small red onion, finely chopped
1 fresh red chili, cored, seeded, and finely chopped
2 tablespoons olive oil
salt and freshly ground black pepper

To peel the tomatoes, cut a cross in the rounded side of each tomato.

Place them in a bowl and pour boiling water over to cover. Leave for 1 minute then drain and cover with cold water. Leave for 1 more minute, then remove and peel. Cut tomatoes into quarters and remove cores, then cut tomato flesh into tiny dice and place in a bowl.

Add olives, onion, and chili to tomatoes in the bowl. Stir in olive oil and season with salt and pepper. Transfer to a serving bowl and serve.

Serves 4

— AVOCADO & MELON SALSA —

1 ripe avocado
½ canteloupe melon
juice 1 lime
4 scallions, very finely chopped
1 fresh red chili, cored, seeded, and very finely
  chopped
salt and freshly ground black pepper
mint leaves, to garnish

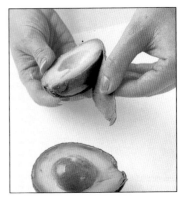

Cut the avocado in half. Remove the stone
and peel off the skin.

Remove seeds from melon and cut away
skin. Cut avocado and melon into small
dice and place in a bowl with lime juice.
Toss together well. Add scallions and chili.
Season with salt and pepper.

Cover closely with plastic wrap and leave to
stand for 30 minutes. (Do not leave for
longer than this or the avocado will
discolor.) Transfer to a serving dish.
Roughly tear or chop the mint leaves and
scatter over the salsa before serving.

Serves 4

VARIATION: Any type of melon can be used
as long as it is ripe and has a good flavor.
You should have 8oz melon after peeling
and seeding.

BEAN SALAD

14oz canned black-eyed beans
14oz canned red kidney beans
4 stalks celery, chopped
1 green bell pepper, seeded and roughly chopped
1 small red onion, finely chopped
4 tablespoons olive oil
1 tablespoon lime juice
1 teaspoon sugar
½-1 teaspoon hot pepper sauce
salt and freshly ground black pepper
2 tablespoons chopped fresh parsley

Drain and rinse black-eyed beans and red kidney beans. Place in a bowl.

Add the celery, green bell pepper, and onion to the beans.

In a bowl, mix together olive oil, lime juice, sugar, and hot pepper sauce. Season with salt and pepper. Pour over the bean mixture and mix well. Set aside for 30 minutes then transfer to a serving dish. Scatter with chopped parsley and serve.

Serves 4-6

VARIATIONS: The combination of beans can be varied according to preference and what is available.

COUSCOUS SALAD

3 tablespoons olive oil
5 scallions, chopped
1 clove garlic, crushed
1 teaspoon ground cumin
1½ cups vegetable stock
1 cup couscous
2 tomatoes, peeled and chopped
4 tablespoons chopped fresh parsley
4 tablespoons chopped fresh mint
1 fresh green chili, cored, seeded, and finely chopped
2 tablespoons lemon juice
salt and freshly ground black pepper
toasted pine nuts and grated lemon rind, to garnish

Heat oil in a saucepan. Add scallions and garlic.

Stir in cumin. Add stock and bring to a boil. Remove the pan from the heat and stir in couscous. Leave to stand for 10 minutes until couscous has absorbed all the liquid. Fluff up with a fork and transfer to a serving dish.

Leave to cool then stir in tomatoes, parsley, mint, chili, and lemon juice. Season with salt and pepper. Leave to stand for up to 1 hour to allow the flavors to develop. Scatter pine nuts and lemon rind over and serve.

Serves 4

– ORANGE & RED ONION SALAD –

6 oranges
2 small red onions
1 tablespoon cumin seeds
1 teaspoon coarsely ground black pepper
1 tablespoon chopped fresh mint
6 tablespoons olive oil
salt
mint sprigs and black olives, to garnish

Working over a bowl to catch the juice, cut the skin away from oranges, removing the pith.

With a sharp knife, slice the oranges thinly. Slice onions across thinly, into rings, then separate the layers of the rings. Arrange the orange and onion slices in layers in a shallow dish. Sprinkle each layer with cumin seeds, black pepper, mint, olive oil, and salt to taste.

Pour any orange juice saved from slicing oranges over the salad. Leave in a cool place for about 2 hours, for the flavors to develop. Just before serving, scatter the salad with mint sprigs and black olives.

Serves 6

VARIATION: Slices of fennel may be added to this salad.

ASIAN GREEN SALAD

4oz snow peas, trimmed and halved
1 small head Chinese leaves
8 scallions, roughly chopped
1 green bell pepper, seeded and sliced
½ small cucumber
2 cups bean sprouts
2 tablespoons chopped roasted cashew nuts, and
  2 tablespoons chopped fresh cilantro, to garnish
DRESSING
1 inch piece fresh root ginger, grated
1 clove garlic, crushed
1 fresh red chili, cored, seeded, and finely chopped
1 teaspoon honey
grated rind and juice 1 lime
2 tablespoons oil
1 tablespoon soy sauce

Bring a pan of water to a boil, add snow peas, cook for 2 minutes, then drain and refresh in cold water. (See above.) Drain again and place in a bowl. Finely shred Chinese leaves and add to the bowl with the scallions and green bell pepper.

Peel cucumber, cut in half lengthwise and slice thinly. Add to the bowl with bean sprouts. To make the dressing, whisk together ginger, garlic, chili, honey, lime rind and juice, oil, and soy sauce. Pour over the salad and mix well. Transfer to a serving bowl. Before serving, scatter over chopped cashew nuts and cilantro.

Serves 4-6

INDEX